BATAAN: THE MARCH OF DEATH

"Excellent ... a model of careful research."
American Historical Review

"This thorough book brings back sharply the events that happened at Bataan."

Washington Star

"Memorable ... well-written ... well-organized."
Publishers Weekly

"A solid contribution to our knowledge of the war ... a story worth reading and remembering."
Washington Post

BATAAN
THE MARCH OF DEATH
STANLEY L. FALK

PLAYBOY
PAPERBACKS

For Lynn

Contents

Illustrations and Maps

Illustrations

*All photographs reproduced through courtesy of the Depart-
ment of Defense.*

Preface

In the spring of 1942, the Japanese 14th Army overran Bataan Peninsula on the island of Luzon in the Philippines and captured 78,100 American and Filipino troops. Almost immediately, a curtain of silence settled over Bataan, concealing from the rest of the world the fate of the prisoners. It was not until more than a year and one-half later that the mystery was dispelled and a shocked America learned of the events that had followed the Japanese victory. Almost immediately, the tragic story of the evacuation of the Filipino and American captives from Bataan became the most publicized episode of the entire Philippine campaign. Marked by brutality and suffering, it was immediately named the "March of Death," or, more simply, the "Death March," and it is as the Death March that it has been known ever since.

The entire story of the Death March has never been told. A few survivors have written about their experiences, and brief, incomplete, and sometimes misleading accounts have also appeared in print. This book attempts for the first time to tell the whole story of what happened after Bataan surrendered, and to tell it from the Japanese side as well as from the viewpoint of the Americans and Filipinos. It is based on American and Japanese army records, on the war crimes trial of Lieutenant General Masaharu Homma, who commanded the Japanese army in the Philippines and who was subsequently executed for his part in these events, on interviews with survivors, on diaries, letters, and personal accounts, and on other hitherto untapped sources.

Most of the research for this book was done in fulfillment of the requirements for a graduate degree at Georgetown University, and I am grateful to that institution for permission to use this material. I am deeply indebted to Professor Louis Morton of Dartmouth College, formerly of the Office, Chief of Military History, Department of the Army, and to the Reverend Joseph T. Durkin, S.J., of Georgetown, both of whom carefully read and criticized my early drafts. Major General Albert M. Jones was also kind enough to read and comment on the manuscript. My most important obligation is to the many officers who gave freely of their time to describe for me, in interviews or letters, their experiences on Bataan, and to permit my use of their personal papers. The use of documents and photographs on file in the Office of Military History is also gratefully acknowledged. And finally, I should like to express my appreciation to my friends and colleagues at the Office of Military History who encouraged, indeed urged, me to write this book.

Stanley L. Falk

Prisoner of War! . . . it is . . . a melancholy state. You are in the power of your enemy. You owe your life to his humanity, and your daily bread to his compassion. You must obey his orders, go where he tells you, stay where you are bid, await his pleasure, possess your soul in patience.

—Winston S. Churchill,
A Roving Commission *

I
The Fall of Bataan

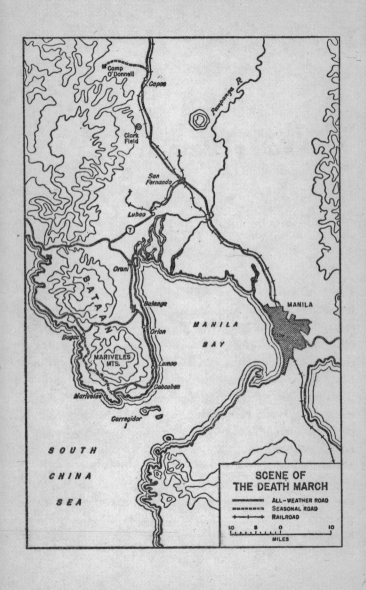

Camp O'Donnell

Capas

Pampanga R.

Clark Field

San Fernando

Lubao

Orani

B A T A A N

Balanga

Orion

Bagac

MARIVELES MTS.

Lamao

Cabcaben

Mariveles

Corregidor I.

MANILA

MANILA BAY

SOUTH

CHINA

SEA

SCENE OF
THE DEATH MARCH

ALL-WEATHER ROAD
SEASONAL ROAD
RAILROAD

10   5   0   10

MILES

1

"The Japanese Are Not Barbarians"

The Japanese had hit southern Bataan with overwhelming force. In less than a week they had shattered and crushed the American and Filipino defenders. As the hot tropical sun finally set on the fifth day of battle, it was clear that continued resistance was useless. Morning could only bring further retreat—and wholesale slaughter.

Major General Edward P. King, Jr., the American commander on Bataan Peninsula, had his orders. Under no circumstances was he to surrender. Yet he now knew that he had no other choice.

Three months of enemy pressure, of starvation and disease, of blockade and bombardment, had left his troops so weak that they could barely fight. For five days now they had unsuccessfully attempted to halt the latest Japanese offensive. Now they no longer had the physical strength to make another effort. No matter what they did, they could not prevent or delay the swift Japanese occupation of the few square miles of Bataan still in American hands.

On King's shoulders rested the responsibility for more than 78,000 American and Filipino soldiers and a third as many civilians. If he surrendered quickly, their lives might yet be saved. If he continued to fight, all would be doomed. Neither course of action would in any way slow the Japanese advance.

Shortly before midnight on the evening of April 8, 1942, King reluctantly concluded that he would have to surrender. Continued resistance could gain no military advantage and would only result in futile bloodshed. Not only were the troops no longer capable of defending themselves, but the American hospitals with their thousands of helpless patients lay unprotected before the Japanese guns. And to underline the hopelessness of the situation, King's quartermaster had only one more half-ration of food to issue to the exhausted troops—if there was still any way left to distribute it. After that had been given out, the Bataan food stocks would be exhausted.

The decision made, King informed his staff. "We have no further means of organized resistance," he told them. At about three-thirty on the morning of April 9th, he sent two of his staff officers forward under a flag of truce to establish contact with the Japanese commander.

The two emissaries, Colonel Everett C. Williams and Major Marshall Hurt, Jr., were charged with arranging a meeting between King and Lieutenant General Masaharu Homma, the Japanese commander in the Philippines. Should

Homma refuse to see King, Williams and Hurt were to ask for surrender terms themselves.

On this point, King gave them very explicit instructions. They were to bring to the attention of the Japanese the weakened condition of his troops and to obtain permission for King to assemble the disorganized units himself and move them in his own vehicles to whatever place the Japanese might designate.

In a letter of instructions for Williams and Hurt, King outlined specific points to be raised for Japanese consideration. In view of what followed, his exact words are worth studying:

a. The large number of sick and wounded in the two general hospitals, particularly Hospital #1 which is dangerously close to the area wherein projectiles may be expected to fall if hostilities continue.

b. The fact that our forces are somewhat disorganized and that it will be quite difficult to assemble them. This assembling and organizing of our own forces, necessary prior to their being delivered as prisoners of war, will necessarily take some time and can be accomplished by my own staff under my direction.

c. The physical condition of the command due to long siege, during which they have been on short rations, which will make it very difficult to move them great distances on foot.

d. In order to assist in this matter, I have issued orders directing the use of motor transportation in assembling and delivering the personnel, to such places as might be directed.

e. Request consideration for the vast number of civilians present at this time in Bataan, most of whom have simply drifted in and whom we have had to feed and care for. These people are in no way connected with the American or Filipino Forces and their presence is simply incidental due to the circumstances under which the Bataan phase of hostilities was precipitated.

19

As Williams and Hurt moved north to meet the Japanese, King notified his major commanders of the impending surrender. They in turn sent word to whatever subordinate commanders they could reach. Soon great explosions began to rock Bataan as tons of military supplies and equipment were blown sky high to keep them from falling into enemy hands. The exploding munitions sent bursting shells and colored flashes of light into the night until southern Bataan resembled a gigantic Fourth of July spectacle.

Meanwhile, Williams and Hurt were having a difficult time reaching the Japanese lines. The road north was jammed with beaten, demoralized soldiers, on foot and in jeeps and trucks, and the two officers were soon forced to abandon their own vehicles and try to go ahead on foot. Neither had any idea of what awaited them to the north, of what sort of reception the Japanese might give them. Major Hurt recalls that he talked to himself, said a few prayers, and tried to imagine what might be in store for him. Colonel Williams was evidently too busy trying to make his way forward through the crush of men and vehicles to do much thinking.

Finally they broke through the traffic jam. The road ahead lay empty and ominously quiet. Commandeering a jeep and a frightened driver, they drove north and just before daylight reached the last American outpost. An hour later, as the sun began to rise, the troops manning this position withdrew and Williams and Hurt pushed forward to meet the Japanese.

Their first sight of the enemy was nearly their last. A platoon of Japanese infantry noticed the jeep and, with fixed bayonets flashing, charged down on the Americans. Williams and Hurt frantically waved a large bedsheet, their improvised

20

white flag of surrender, and then cautiously got out with their hands raised. Only the arrival of a Japanese officer at this time saved the mission, for the Japanese soldiers neither understood nor seemed to care about the fact that Williams and Hurt bore a surrender message from General King.

Accompanied by the Japanese officer, the two Americans soon found themselves in the presence of Major General Kameichiro Nagano, the commander of the enemy force moving down Bataan's east coast. Fortunately for the Americans, Nagano had an interpreter on hand, and for the first time King's emissaries were able to explain their mission. After a brief discussion, Nagano agreed to meet the American commander near the town of Lamao. Nothing was said about a meeting with Homma. Instead, the Japanese sent Major Hurt back to get King. Colonel Williams was held at Nagano's headquarters.

As soon as General King learned what had happened, he selected three men—Colonel James V. Collier, his operations officer, and Major Wade Cothran and Captain Achile C. Tisdale, his two aides—to accompany him and Major Hurt to the meeting with Nagano. At a few minutes after nine, wearing his last clean uniform and feeling like Lee on his way to meet Grant at Appomattox, King set out with the others from his command post.

As the five men drove north to meet the Japanese, the white flag of surrender flew sadly above them and cast its bitter shadow across the road. In a few short hours, they believed, the horrors of Bataan would be ended.

Whatever thoughts of the future were on King's mind, he had little time to consider them. Hardly had the two jeeps carrying his party left the American command post, when Japanese planes swooped low to bomb and strafe them. King and the others frantically waved their white flags and, when this had no effect, pulled their jeeps to a halt and flung themselves into a ditch. Time after time they returned to the two vehicles, drove forward a few hundred yards, and then were forced to take cover as the Japanese planes attacked again. It was nearly eleven o'clock before these attacks ceased and the five Americans were able to continue their ride. When they reached the first Japanese outpost, they had been traveling for two hours and had covered a distance of about three miles.

Still shaken from their trip, King and his party were led by Japanese soldiers to a group of chairs set around a small table in front of a Filipino farmhouse. Here King had hoped to meet General Homma. Instead, he was told, the Japanese commander would send one of his officers. Homma himself would not see King.

The Americans had been seated for only a few minutes when a shiny black Cadillac drew up before the farmhouse. From it, amidst a great deal of saluting and bowing, stepped two Japanese. The first was Colonel Motoo Nakayama, Homma's senior operations officer, a short, brusque, unsmiling man. The other was his interpreter.

As King rose to greet the Japanese, Nakayama ignored him and took a seat across the table from the general. King resumed his own chair, sitting straight up, his hands thrust forward before him. Captain Tisdale, seated beside the general, recalled later that he had never seen him "look more like a soldier."

The conference immediately got off to a bad start. Nakayama, stiffly erect in his own chair, fixed his eyes on King and asked sharply: "You are General Wainwright?" Lieutenant General Jonathan M. Wainwright was King's superior, the commander of all American and Filipino forces in the Philippines. King had come to surrender Bataan, but it was obvious that Nakayama thought he was Wainwright surrendering all of the Philippines.

Slowly and patiently through the Japanese interpreter, King explained his position. No, he was not General Wainwright, nor did he speak for him. No, he had not come to surrender everything in the Philippines, only Bataan.

Nakayama was obviously angry. "Go and get Wainwright," he said. The Japanese would accept no surrender without him.

Again King explained his position. Again he said that he wished to surrender Bataan, that he had no control over the rest of the Philippines, and that he certainly had no power to bring Wainwright to Nakayama. It was some time before he could persuade the Japanese to listen to his offer to surrender.

Once he had made clear his status, King explained that he could no longer put up any organized resistance and that he wanted an armistice to halt further bloodshed. His troops, he said, were not only completely scattered and demoralized, but they were also sick, starving, and exhausted. If the Japanese would grant it to him, he wanted time to reorganize his forces and reform them into units, under their own officers, for evacuation from Bataan. King had saved enough vehicles and gasoline, he pointed out, to deliver his entire force to any assembly point that General Homma desired.

Primarily concerned about the treatment his men would receive, General King tried repeatedly to secure a guarantee that the provisions of the Geneva Convention for the treatment of prisoners would be carried out. Again and again he pleaded for assurance that the American and Filipino soldiers would be regarded as prisoners of war under the terms of the Convention. But he had little luck.

Colonel Nakayama refused to make any conditions. Since King did not speak for Wainwright and could not surrender the entire Philippine garrison, it was "absolutely impossible," said Nakayama, to negotiate for the surrender of Bataan. The troops on Bataan could give up if they wished. But, he declared, it would have to be by individual unit, "voluntarily and unconditionally!"

As King listened hopelessly to Nakayama's stern words, he could hear the sounds of fighting still continuing. The boom of Japanese artillery, the rattle of small arms, the roar of Japanese planes as they swooped to bomb and strafe the helpless defenders—all made it painfully clear to him that he had no choice. Each moment he delayed meant the death of more of his men. At about half past twelve he told Nakayama that he would surrender unconditionally.

With an impatient gesture of triumph, the Japanese demanded General King's sword. This unexpected reversion to a bygone form of military etiquette flabbergasted King. He had left his sword in Manila at the outbreak of the war and in the heat and dust of the fighting on Bataan had not thought of it for months. Again he had to make a lengthy explanation to Nakayama. Again the Japanese colonel was angry and incredulous. Finally, however, King persuaded Nakayama to accept his pistol.

The general placed his weapon on the table before him. The other Americans did the same with their pistols. The conference was ended. They were prisoners of the Japanese.

Exhausted by the difficult negotiations, King was further depressed because he had been unable to secure the conditions he had hoped for. Still, he believed that he had surrendered his entire force. Yet even in this he was mistaken.

Colonel Nakayama viewed King's surrender as that of a single officer to General Nagano, the local commander, and no signed statement of formal capitulation was executed. "The surrender," wrote Nakayama after the war, "was accomplished by the voluntary and unconditional surrender of each individual or each unit. The negotiations for the cessation of hostilities failed."

It is doubtful, however, that a written surrender document would in any way have altered the events that followed. General King had done all that he could, but he had been unable to secure a pledge from the Japanese that the prisoners would be well treated. The only response to his repeated insistence on this point was a single curt assertion by General Homma's representative.

"The Imperial Japanese Army," declared Colonel Nakayama, "are not barbarians."

2

The Battling Bastards

General King's decision to surrender came but four months and one day after the Japanese attack on Pearl Harbor. On that fateful 8th of December in 1941—the 7th, Hawaiian time—when the attention of the world was drawn suddenly to the great American naval base in the mid-Pacific, the Japanese had not neglected the Philippines. Here, too, their bombers had struck with crippling force. In the burning wreckage of the American Far East Air Force at Clark Field, as in the sunken hulks of the Pacific Fleet at Pearl Harbor, was sealed the fate of the men who surrendered on Bataan four months later.

Within two weeks of the first day of war, the Japanese achieved air and naval supremacy in the Philippines and isolated the forces under General Douglas MacArthur from the rest of the world. MacArthur's troops, consisting for the most part of the newly mobilized Philippine Army, were now cut off from supply or reinforcement and would have to fight it out on their own.

A few days before Christmas, the bulk of the Japanese 14th Army landed on Luzon, largest and northernmost of the Philippine Islands. General Homma's well-trained, veteran troops poured ashore against only slight resistance and immediately launched a drive on the capital city of Manila. The defenders, hastily organized, poorly equipped, and ill-prepared, were no match for the invaders.

It was obvious to MacArthur that a pitched battle with the Japanese would quickly bring about the total destruction of his command. Such a rapid disaster would deliver to General Homma the prize he sought in the briefest of time and allow the Japanese to continue unimpeded their drive south to the Indies.

To prevent anything like this from happening, MacArthur decided on a bold course. He would pull his troops back to the shelter of Bataan, a small mountainous, jungle peninsula that juts out into the mouth of Manila Bay. From here there was no way out, no escape. Every single one of the defenders would be doomed to death or capture. But so long as MacArthur and his men could hold out, so long would General Homma be denied the entrance to the fine harbor of Manila. And without the port of Manila, the Japanese timetable for the capture of the Indies might well be drastically delayed.

By the first days of the new year, within two weeks of his decision to fall back to Bataan, MacArthur had successfully completed his withdrawal. Through the bitter months of January, February, and March, under mounting pressure, his troops held the Japanese. April 3rd, Good Friday of 1942, found the defenders back on their final line in southern Bataan, a line from which there was no retreat.

The final position for the Bataan defenders stretched about fifteen miles across the waist of the peninsula, from the west coast town of Bagac, on the South China Sea, to the village of Orion, on the shores of Manila Bay. North of the Bagac-Orion line stood the Japanese, blocking the route of escape. In all other directions was the sea.

South of Bataan, guarding the vital entrance to Manila Bay, lay the tiny fortified island of Corregidor and its three even smaller sister islets. Who held Corregidor controlled Manila Bay, but who held Bataan controlled Corregidor. For overshadowing southern Bataan, safely protected by the Bagac-Orion line, was a huge extinct volcanic mass, the Mariveles Mountains, which rose to a height of nearly a mile. Artillery emplaced on the southern slopes of this rugged mass could dominate the island fortress and render it untenable. Southern Bataan was thus a prize to be defended to the death and, for the Japanese, to be captured at all costs.

In the approximately 200 square miles of Bataan Peninsula still denied to the Japanese were crowded over 100,000 people. More than 78,000 troops made up the bulk of this population, but there were also some 6,000 civilian employees of the Army and about 20,000 Filipino refugees who had sought shelter in southern Bataan. Here too were crowded whatever supplies and equipment the battered defenders had managed to carry to their last retreat, artillery, tanks, and other vehicles, gasoline and oil stocks, and precious stores of ammunition and food. Scattered also throughout the area were the command posts, hospitals, communications centers, and all of the other vital installations needed to keep an army fighting.

"Bataan was so crowded," recalled one American staff officer, "that bombers could drop their pay loads at almost any point or place and hit something of military value."

In the middle of March, President Roosevelt had ordered General MacArthur south to Australia. His departure left the command of the embattled Philippine garrison to General Wainwright. From his headquarters on Corregidor, Wainwright commanded all the troops in the entire Philippine archipelago, of which the forces on Bataan constituted the single most important part. Wainwright's commander on Bataan, elevated to that position late in March, was General King.

Quiet, courteous, capable, a veteran artilleryman with a law degree from the University of Georgia and a well-deserved reputation as a soldier, King assumed command on Bataan less than three weeks before he was forced to surrender. He understood the inevitable tragedy of his position and bore his cross unflinchingly.

King's command was known as the Luzon Force, a weary army of Filipinos led by and built around a cadre of Americans. This army was organized into two corps. The I Philippine Corps, commanded by Major General Albert M. Jones, held the western portion of the Bagac-Orion line. The II Philippine Corps, under Major General George M. Parker, Jr., defended the eastern half of the position. Both corps commanders were able, energetic soldiers. But, like General King, neither had any illusions about the future.

Of the 78,100 troops on Bataan, more than 66,000 were

Philippine nationals, most of whom had been hastily mobilized and inducted into the American Army in the few months just before the war. These Filipinos were organized into seven Philippine Army divisions, one Philippine Constabulary division, and three Philippine Scout regiments of the regular U.S. Army.

American soldiers made up less than 15 per cent of the Luzon Force, and they were widely scattered. Some led or "advised" Filipino units; others performed vital staff and command work. The remainder constituted the few units on Bataan composed entirely of Americans, only one of which, the 31st Infantry Regiment, was a regular U.S. Army outfit. There were also two American tank battalions and a number of improvised infantry units composed of Air Corps troops and sailors.

None of the units of the Luzon Force was up to its authorized strength. Few were sufficiently trained or disciplined for the trials of combat. But these inadequacies, while pressing, were still relatively minor problems. For overshadowing all other considerations on Bataan was the shortage of food and medicine. Ultimately, it would decide the fate of the Luzon Force.

General MacArthur's decision to withdraw to Bataan had completed the isolation of the Luzon garrison from all sources of supply except via a tenuous line through the ever-tightening Japanese blockade. All that the defenders of Bataan had to fight with and exist on was what they themselves had managed to transport to the peninsula before General Homma slammed the doors shut behind them.

The Filipino and American troops had gone into Bataan,

in the words of one Japanese officer, "like a cat entering a sack." There was no way out, and the men would have to do with what they had.

Dramatic recognition of the plight of the Bataan defenders came but a few days after they had reached that jungled peninsula. The number of troops and civilians, well over 100,000 people, roughly equaled the population of present-day Allentown, Pennsylvania. But the amount of food on Bataan would feed a city this size for only thirty days. On January 5th, then, MacArthur ordered the daily food ration cut in half, an order that was never revoked.

The half-ration decreed by MacArthur would theoretically provide an American with thirty-six ounces of food each day, and a Filipino with thirty-two ounces. Actually, neither ever received as much as thirty after the end of January. And since each day's ration was determined solely by the amount of food actually on hand, no one got the same portion each day.

By mid-February, the Filipino and American troops were being issued only 27.7 ounces of food per day. In the weeks that followed, the ration was further cut, until by the 5th of March the daily issue amounted to less than fifteen ounces, smaller than one-quarter of the normal peacetime ration. During the months before General King's surrender, the hungry troops were eating just enough food to sustain life, but little more.

Rice, the basic food of the Orient, was the main item of the ration. For the American soldier, raised on bread and potatoes, it was unappealing and distasteful. Unlike the Filipino, for whom rice was the staple, the American found that it tasted like "wallpaper paste." To add anything at all to rice was to improve it. White, gummy, and tasteless, it helped to fill his stomach, but it never satisfied him.

With his rice, the soldier had little else to eat, so that his diet was uninteresting and monotonous. Items like butter, coffee, and tea—normally regarded by Americans as necessities—soon disappeared, and canned vegetables, sugar, and canned milk were so scarce that the men regarded them as luxuries. By the end of March, the daily ration totalled but eight and one-half ounces of rice, an ounce and one-half each of flour and salt, slightly less of canned meat and milk, and barely half an ounce of sugar.

If supplies could not somehow reach the hungry Bataan defenders, General Wainwright radioed desperately to Washington, "the troops there will be starved into submission."

Many attempts were made to increase the food supply, but few were successful. Almost every effort to run the Japanese blockade ended in tragic and disappointing failure. Months of endeavor resulted in the arrival of only one week's issue, hardly enough to have any real effect on the stunted ration.

The troops also made valiant efforts to exploit the slim resources of the embattled peninsula, but Bataan had little to offer. Two rice mills constructed to thresh the unhusked rice which might be gathered in the narrow rice belt along the east coast worked well until there was no more rice to be gathered. Yet the end result was less than a seventeen-day supply under the cut ration. Another effort was made by local fisherman, and for a while they hauled in a small but welcome catch each night. But Japanese and misdirected American gunfire brought an end to these nocturnal expeditions.

Until the stock of fresh meat was exhausted, the Luzon Force quartermaster issued some about twice a week. The Philippine beast of burden, the carabao, was the principal source of this supply, and in the absence of refrigeration the animals were kept in stockyards and slaughtered as close as possible to the time the meat was to be issued. Many carabao, roaming wild or the property of some unfortunate Filipino farmer, were seized and killed by the hungry troops themselves. Despite orders to the contrary from MacArthur—who feared that this unauthorized slaughter would lead to the consumption of diseased meat and the reduction of fresh meat stocks for regular issue—roughly 1,000 carabao were killed and eaten by amateur butchers amongst the troops.

The only other source of fresh meat was provided by the 250 horses and forty-eight pack mules of the 26th Cavalry Regiment, but this supply was exhausted by mid-March.

Hunger made great foragers of the Filipino soldiers, who soon learned to secure from Bataan and its tiny villages such delicacies as pigs, chickens, sweet potatoes, bananas, mangoes, and tender young bamboo shoots. Dog and monkey meat, the chicken-like flesh of the iguana lizard, and the meat and eggs of the deadly python were also prey for the ingenious hunter. And soldiers on patrol, ostensibly seeking human game, would often gather rice standing unpicked in nearby fields and then laboriously thresh the grain in their individual foxholes.

Nor were such additions to the daily menu ignored by the American troops, no less hungry than their Filipino comrades. Colonel Richard C. Mallonée, an American artilleryman, prepared a diners' guide to items outside the regular ration. "I can recommend mule," he wrote in his diary after a representative sampling. "It is tasty, succulent, and tender —all being phrases of comparison, of course. There is little to choose between calesa pony and carabao. Iguana is fair. Monkey I do not recommend."

But General King's aide, Captain Tisdale, a little further back from the front lines, complained sadly that "monkeys and iguana are quite scarce and about all we have is rice."

There were other ways of supplementing the inadequate ration. Hungry, desperate men thought nothing of stopping and looting supply trucks, often at gunpoint. Even the truckdrivers were not above helping themselves to some of the cargo entrusted to them. Often, however, supply trucks were targets for Japanese air or artillery bombardment, or enemy attacks on other targets halted the movement of fresh meat until it had rotted in the hot Bataan sun.

To assure a fair distribution of food, all units were ordered to turn in excess rations picked up at depots during the withdrawal to Bataan. Few, however, complied. As a result, many had their own small, but private, supply dumps. Other units drew extra food on the basis of padded strength reports, and at one time this practice was so widespread that the 78,100 soldiers on Bataan were being issued rations for 122,000 men. "It appears," reported one supply officer with considerable restraint, "that many units are doubling up."

But the gains from such practices were not enough to raise the food level of the individual soldier. All they served to do was to provide an uneven ration for the troops, and, as is usually the case in war, the men closest to the fighting were the most distant from the supply dumps—and suffered accordingly.

As a result, some men ate corned beef, others accounted themselves lucky with fish, still others got neither. Eight ounces of rice were issued to some soldiers; troops in other units received half as much. Sometimes an outfit on the move would miss a whole day's ration, or, as often, would draw a double issue. But if the daily ration for all the troops on Bataan had one thing in common, it could only be its inadequacy.

The plight of the individual soldier seemed even worse when he found himself without a smoke. And this was most of the time. During the three months they were besieged on Bataan, the Filipino and American troops received an average of less than one cigarette a day. Heavy smokers suffered intensely. They gladly paid five dollars for a five cent pack of cigarettes, and thanked the seller for dealing with them. Men who would pounce on any discarded cigarette butt in hope of getting a few puffs of precious smoke were not liable to complain about excess profits on the tobacco black market. Commanders worried about morale but, like most other supply questions, the problem of cigarettes defied solution.

The scarcity of clothing and individual equipment also contributed to the wretchedness of each soldier. Threadbare uniforms, worn-out shoes, shabby blankets when he could get them, raincoats, and tents offered a man little protection against the thorns and thickets of the Bataan jungles and shielded him even less against the hot tropical sun and cold Philippine nights. Clothing replacement was almost unavailable and even hospital patients gave up their uniforms to clothe the men at the front.

Poorly clothed and worse fed, the American and Filipino troops were ready victims for still another enemy, disease. The earliest and most readily apparent illnesses were those arising from malnutrition and vitamin deficiency. An active soldier needs 3,500 to 4,000 calories daily. Yet in January, the men received about 2,000 calories a day, three-quarters of that in February, and in March only 1,000 calories. Combined with the absence of necessary vitamins, this caloric insufficiency soon brought alarming results. Diarrhea, dysentery, and the first signs of beriberi became the lot of most of the troops. Night blindness, swellings, and other nutritional illnesses were also common. The sunken cheeks and wasted bodies of the hungry provided universal evidence of dangerous muscle waste and loss of fat reserve.

So low was the men's resistance to disease that the Luzon Force medical officer, Lieutenant Colonel Harold W. Glattly, warned General King in late March that any sickness might easily become an epidemic.

Malaria was the most common disease. The shortage of quinine increased its spread among the troops deployed in the low, anopheles-infested valley north of the Mariveles Mountains. Preventive doses of the drug were halted at the end of February to preserve enough for those already stricken, and within a week the number of daily malaria admissions to the hospital jumped to 500. By the end of March, this figure had reached the almost unbelievable amount of 1,000, and at least three-quarters of the troops at the front had malaria to some degree or other. Attempts to bring quinine through the Japanese blockade were for the most part unsuccessful. On the 1st of April there remained less than one week's supply with which to treat the stricken.

The poor sanitary conditions in Philippine Army units contributed further to the spread of disease. Few of the Filipinos had received adequate training in hygienic measures, and most acted accordingly. They drank unboiled water, failed to clean their mess kits, buried garbage improperly if they bothered to bury it at all, and either built poor latrines or did without them. Huge black flies swarmed about the messy kitchen areas, and other germ-bearing insects were attracted in great numbers.

"Sanitation," noted Colonel Mallonée in his diary, "was ghastly. Straddle trenches—when built—adjoined kitchens. . . . The calls of nature were responded to when and where heard." It is small wonder that diarrhea, dysentery, and, among the often barefooted Filipinos, hookworm were common diseases on Bataan. The shortage of medicine made it impossible to check their spread.

The growth of disease was a grave strain on the capacity and resources of the two Bataan hospitals, General Hospital No. 1, on the southeast slopes of the Mariveles Mountains, and General Hospital No. 2, a few miles away near the town of Cabcaben on the east coast. Built to accommodate 1,000 patients apiece, each was soon caring for more than 3,000. When the sick rate continued to rise, it was necessary to limit admission to patients who either required serious surgical treatment or whose recovery was expected to take more than three weeks.

All but the most seriously ill or wounded patients were turned away to clearing stations or collecting companies, originally intended to provide only emergency treatment to casualties. Yet the end of March found more than 11,000 patients in the two general hospitals and an additional, provisional hospital set up in the I Corps area. Medical facilities at lower echelons were equally overcrowded. By the first week in April, there may have been as many as 24,000 sick and wounded in hospitals and aid stations on Bataan.

Hunger and disease reduced the combat efficiency of General King's troops at an alarming rate. As early as mid-March, the effectiveness of the men in the II Corps appeared to be barely 20 per cent of normal, with that of I Corps troops only slightly better. By the 1st of April, the Luzon Force was but a shell of an effective fighting command, its combat efficiency, reported King, "rapidly approaching the zero point."

When the Japanese began their final offensive, the Filipino and American troops who held the line from Bagac to Orion were already defeated. With empty stomachs and sick bodies, with minds tortured by the strain of fighting and the knowledge that all hope of aid from the outside was gone, the Bataan defenders were completely incapable of making and maintaining the physical effort necessary for the struggle. Only their spirit, a last spark of defiance, kept them fighting.

Their grim feeling of jaunty hopelessness found expression in these brief lines, the battle cry of the hungry and exhausted men:

> We're the battling bastards of Bataan;
> No mama, no papa, no Uncle Sam;
> No aunts, no uncles, no cousins, no nieces;
> No pills, no planes, no artillery pieces.
> . . . And nobody gives a damn.

3

The Good Friday Offensive

On the other side of the Bagac-Orion line, the Japanese were unaware of the desperate condition of the Bataan defenders. Indeed, even as General King was vainly preparing for the enemy offensive he knew must come, General Homma was carefully building up the strength of the 14th Army. Elsewhere in the Pacific, Japanese forces had been overwhelmingly successful, and Imperial General Headquarters in Tokyo was becoming increasingly unhappy about the stalemate in the Philippines. Already Homma had received strong indications that any further delay might mean his relief from command. The Bataan defenders would have to be finished off, he was told—and quickly.

During March, then, steady Japanese reinforcements poured into the Philippines: a division from Shanghai, a regimental combat team diverted from Indo-China, heavy artillery units from Hong Kong, and heavy bombers from

Malaya, as well as thousands of individual replacements. With this added strength, Homma no longer had any excuse for failure. He had ample fresh troops, plenty of guns and planes, and, he believed, a total numerical advantage of nearly two to one over King.

Yet the Japanese commander was worried. The spirited Filipino-American stand on Bataan had given him a healthy respect for the defenders. How could he be certain they would not spring some new trick on him? "I do not know," he wrote in his diary, "whether the enemy on Bataan will try to fight to the end . . . whether they will retreat back to Corregidor and fight, escape to Australia . . . or give up at the right time. But I still propose to prepare for the worst."

After carefully considering the matter, General Homma and his staff cautiously estimated that it would take about a month to defeat the Filipino-American forces still left on Bataan. To their surprise, the end would come much sooner.

On April 3, 1942, Good Friday, the Japanese opened their attack against the Bagac-Orion line. On the heels of a tremendous air and artillery barrage that shook the whole southern half of Bataan and sent great clouds of dust and smoke swirling to the sky, the whole weight of the 14th Army struck the exhausted defenders. The main attack smashed at the center of General King's line and quickly broke through. A secondary attack pushed back his right flank.

By the evening of Easter Sunday, two Philippine Army divisions of the II Corps had been overwhelmed and scattered. A counterattack by Scouts and American troops had been thrown back. King was forced into a vain attempt to establish another defensive line to halt the powerful Japanese advance.

On April 7th and 8th, the remnants of the II Corps in eastern Bataan repeatedly tried to set up a line along which they might hold. But each time the weak and exhausted defenders sought to stand, they were struck again by the Japanese and forced back. And each time they lost more and more of their organization as a fighting force.

From Orion the line had been thrown south four miles to Limay, and from Limay another three and one-half miles back to Lamao. By the evening of the 8th, the Corps had disintegrated into chaos. Feeble attempts were being made to establish a final defensive line at Cabcaben, another four and one-half miles south, but there was little chance that this could be held against the onrushing enemy. Completely worn out from starvation, disease, and days of ceaseless bombardment, the Bataan defenders were now physically incapable of halting the Japanese.

In the brief span of five days, General Homma had split and outflanked the Luzon Force lines and won undisputed passage to the south. All of Bataan lay at his mercy.

As darkness settled over the embattled peninsula, it was grimly evident to General King that the Luzon Force could not survive another day. A few hours later, with a heavy heart and a dry mouth, he made his tragic decision to surrender.

II
The Best Laid Plans

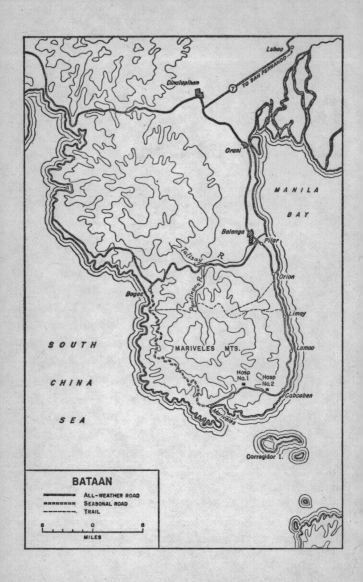

MILES

BATAAN

ALL-WEATHER ROAD
SEASONAL ROAD
TRAIL

4

An Urgent Solution

The fall of Bataan ended all organized resistance on Luzon. The guns were still and silence fell over the peninsula. But for the Japanese it was not the end of the fight, for there, across the waters of Manila Bay, guarding its entrance, stood Corregidor. And so long as it remained in American hands, the fine harbor of Manila, the most valuable prize in the Philippines, was still denied to the conquerors.

Obviously, General Homma must have Corregidor. And he must have it as soon as possible to satisfy his impatient superiors in Tokyo. For if the stubborn American defense on Bataan had not already endangered Homma's career, any further delay in seizing Corregidor would certainly bring it to an inglorious end. He would not be the first officer relieved for failing to meet a timetable set by Imperial General Headquarters.

The clear necessity for a quick victory over Corregidor

ruled out any prolonged attempt to starve the island fortress into submission. A siege like that might take months, and Homma had already spent too much time and too many Japanese lives to wait that long. Clearly he would have to mount an assault as quickly as he could.

There was an old saying in the Japanese army: "After victory, tighten your helmet strings"—do not relax when the battle is won, but be prepared to press on to further victories. In April, 1942, General Homma could not afford to loosen his helmet strings. He could not relax until he had captured Corregidor.

Under these circumstances, the disposition of the American and Filipino troops captured on Bataan was an incidental and relatively unimportant problem. "Though the question required urgent solution," recalled Homma in 1945, "my first and last concern was how I could assault the impregnable fortress [of Corregidor] in the shortest time possible."

Only one thing was important about the prisoners. They were in the way on Bataan and would have to be moved before the Japanese could attack Corregidor.

The reason for this is clear. If troops of the 14th Army were to assemble in southern Bataan for the Corregidor attack, if they were to rest and recover from the strain of combat, if they were to train and practice for an amphibious assault and for the type of combat expected once ashore— then they must have ample room for these activities. Bivouac sites would have to be cleared, maneuver areas selected and marked off, artillery batteries dispersed, camouflaged, and dug in, and many other important operations carried out. The more than 100,000 Americans and Filipinos crowded into southern Bataan would not leave much space for this. Nor would the plans and preparations for the Corregidor assault remain secret for long in the presence of so many enemy troops and sympathizers. When the Japanese-controlled Manila radio was announcing that Corregidor would be captured by "nothing more than blockade"—in an attempt to lull the defenders into lowering their guard—it would hardly do to have such a large number of witnesses to the 14th Army assault preparations.

From the viewpoint of the prisoners themselves, there was still another reason why they should be quickly evacuated from Bataan. So long as they remained there, they would be exposed to American artillery fire from Corregidor. Or, equally undesirable, they would inhibit the Corregidor defenders from firing at Bataan, for fear of hitting their comrades in arms. How much the Japanese considered this, if they thought about it at all, is problematical. But one thing is clear. For both prisoners and captors, it was imperative that none but Japanese remain in southern Bataan.

General Homma had anticipated this problem and had already made his plans. In March, while most of his staff was concentrating on the forthcoming Good Friday offensive, Homma directed the five officers who would have most to do with evacuating the prisoners to begin planning for this movement. The first of these officers was Major General Yoshikata Kawane, the 14th Army transportation officer, who would be responsible for providing transportation for the captives. Homma's second choice was Colonel Toshimitsu Takatsu, his staff officer for administration and logistics. Major Moriya Wada, Colonel Takatsu's assistant for supplies and administration, was the third man. The 14th Army medical department was represented by Major Hisashi Sekiguchi. And a first lieutenant who commanded the Army's "well-digging unit" completed the roster of planners.

On March 23rd, ten days before the final Japanese attack began, the five officers completed their plan and submitted it to General Homma. With his approval, it was put in the form of an order by Major Wada and, two days later, issued with the general directive for the Good Friday offensive.

The plan for handling the prisoners was simple and, on the surface, generally well conceived. It was divided into two phases and the execution of each charged to a different officer. The first phase, a short one, would cover the assembly of all the captured troops and their organization for movement to an internment camp in central Luzon. This would be Colonel Takatsu's responsibility. The second phase, under General Kawane, would take considerably longer and would cover the actual journey of the prisoners to the camp.

Colonel Takatsu's job was to assemble all the captives at the little town of Balanga, about five miles above the eastern anchor of the Bagac-Orion line. Balanga was a logical assembly point, for it stood astride the main road leading out of Bataan. This avenue was called the East Road, a blacktop and in some places gravel road that ran along the coast of Manila Bay from the northern entrance of Bataan to the town of Mariveles at its southern tip. Here it turned north again to follow the coast of western Bataan; this portion, not as well surfaced, was called the West Road. The only other good road was a narrow belt of rough gravel across the waist of the peninsula, linking the East and West Roads. It extended from Bagac, on the west, to Pilar, a town on Manila Bay about a mile below Balanga.

Thus, prisoners taken in western Bataan were to be moved north along the West Road to an initial assembly point at Bagac. From there they would cross the peninsula to Pilar and then turn north to Balanga. Prisoners captured in eastern Bataan would move up the East Road. Those taken in the interior of the peninsula would follow the many winding trails that crisscrossed southern Bataan until they had reached the coast and one of the main roads. Eventually, all the captives would end up in Balanga.

This phase of the evacuation plan did not require any organized movement or line of march. The prisoners could move along in small or large groups and set their own pace. The important thing was to get them the relatively short distance from points in southern Bataan to Balanga, where the Americans and Filipinos could be fed and organized for the movement north out of the peninsula.

The Japanese made no provision for transportation for the prisoners in the first phase of the evacuation. The furthest anyone would have to march would be about twenty-five miles, and most would have a much shorter distance to cover. On April 3rd, for instance, before the Good Friday offensive shattered the Luzon Force line, the 91st Philippine Army Division, dug in below Bagac on the west coast, was fifteen road miles from Balanga. The 11th Philippine Army Division, in central Bataan, was little more than half that distance from Balanga. And the 31st Philippine Army Infantry Regiment, at Orion, was less than five miles from Balanga. The unit that was farthest away, the 57th Philippine

Scout Infantry Regiment, at Mariveles, was twenty-five miles distant on the East Road. The average march for the prisoners would probably be about fifteen miles.

The Japanese Army of World War II did not pamper its soldiers. The normal way for a unit to move from place to place was on foot. Vehicles and gasoline were too precious to waste on men perfectly capable of walking. For many years, Japanese military training had stressed marching and the ability to make long hikes. An American officer who spent six months with the Japanese infantry before the war reported that one day "we started out at five in the morning and marched almost continuously until ten the next morning. In that time we covered fifty-six miles." On another occasion, returning from a twenty-five mile hike in "burning heat," the Japanese troops were not dismissed but instead were ordered to run around the training field two or three times. Their commander explained that he was proving to his men that "they have lots of go and are not as tired as they think they are."

This harsh training paid off in combat, when Japanese troops frequently marched long distances at fairly good speed. Even in heavy jungle and over terrain considered impassable, units burdened by weapons and equipment covered as much as ten to twelve miles a day. Under normal conditions, traveling on reasonably good roads, a Japanese soldier was expected to be able to hike fifteen to twenty-five miles a day—and to maintain this pace for several days. He might be required to march a good deal further under unusual circumstances.

Since the maximum of twenty-five miles that the Filipino

and American prisoners were expected to march was no more than the usual day's march for a Japanese soldier in good condition, the 14th Army planners did not consider this an excessively long walk for their captives.

In the American Army, much more liberally supplied with vehicles and fuel, the normal day's march did not exceed twenty miles except when absolutely necessary. It is doubtful that 14th Army officers were sufficiently acquainted with United States Army practices to be aware of this. But whether they were or not, the average distance the captives were expected to walk was still well under twenty miles.

The Geneva Prisoner of War Convention set the normal day's march at twenty kilometers (twelve and one-half miles), "unless the necessity of reaching water and food depots required longer stages." Whether General Homma's staff considered this is not clear, but in any event the first food depot for the captives was at Balanga.

The Japanese did not plan to feed their prisoners until they had reached the assembly point at Balanga. To attempt to distribute food to a large, disorganized body of troops spread all over the jungle mountains of southern Bataan would have been extremely impractical, if not actually foolish. It would have raised a serious logistical problem and obviously would have required some sort of assembling of the prisoners anyway. It was a lot easier, the Japanese concluded, to bring the prisoners to the food than the other way around.

The Japanese assumed that all the captives could be brought together at Balanga in a day or less. There they would be issued food. Even if many of the prisoners needed more than a single day to get to Balanga, the 14th Army planners expected that they would have enough of their own rations left to sustain them until the first distribution of food.

The initial phase of the evacuation plan was a brief one. Once Colonel Takatsu had assembled the prisoners at the southern end of Balanga, he would form them into groups for the movement north. Here his responsibility ceased.

Now the captives were General Kawane's problem. From Balanga until they reached the prisoner of war camp in central Luzon where they would be interned, the Filipino and American troops would be in his hands. It was his job to feed them, to take care of their sick and wounded, and to provide transportation, if it was available, for moving them.

The Japanese planned to give the prisoners the same type and quantity of food that they issued to their own troops. For this purpose, even before the fall of Bataan, Kawane began assembling rations at four towns along the proposed route of march for the captives. Balanga was the first of these towns. The prisoners would be given a chance to eat here before they began the sixty-five mile trip to their final destination.

The next feeding point above Balanga was the town of Orani, about eight miles away at the base of Bataan peninsula. From here the prisoners would leave Bataan and push north along Route 7 to Lubao, a town in central Luzon about fifteen road miles from Orani, where they would again be fed. Eight miles further to the northeast, at San Fernando, the captives would have their last meal before they reached the internment camp, a short train ride to the north. Prisoners traveling by truck to San Fernando might not have to make any stops after they had left Balanga. But those who were marching would presumably halt for the night at each town where they stopped for food.

To care for the sick and wounded among his captives, General Kawane planned to establish two field hospitals along the route. Ideally, each could accommodate from 500 to 1,000 patients. The first would be at Balanga, well placed to treat the prisoners as soon as they were assembled. The second would be at San Fernando, presumably for any treatment necessary before the final lap of the trip. The staff and equipment for a third hospital was expected from Japan and, if they arrived on time, they would also be used for treating the prisoners. Smaller medical units and aid stations were to treat Filipino and American patients if necessary and rest areas with water and sanitary facilities were to be prepared every mile or so along the route. And finally, those Luzon Force troops already in their own hospitals were to be left there.

While the Japanese plan called for the prisoners to move on foot as far as Balanga, it did not specify just how the captives would travel the thirty-one miles from that point to San Fernando. There was no railroad on Bataan and it was apparent to 14th Army planners almost from the start that most of the Luzon Force troops would have to walk. If General Kawane "had cars," said Homma's chief of staff after the war, "he would use the cars, and if he didn't he would make them march."

The Japanese Army in World War II was not a highly motorized force, and the number of vehicles available to the 14th Army was decidedly limited. Still smaller was the number that could be spared from normal operations for the movement of prisoners. "We estimated," recalled Major Wada, one of the planners, "that if everything went well approximately one-fourth of them could be moved by vehicle." At least 75 per cent of the captives, then, were expected to walk from Balanga to San Fernando.

Above San Fernando the problem was a simple one, for the town was an important junction on the main rail line. This railroad had been partially destroyed by the retreating Filipino and American forces, but the Japanese had restored it in March. There was also ample rolling stock to carry the prisoners. From San Fernando they would ride north about twenty-five miles to the town of Capas, from which point it was another nine-mile hike to the internment camp selected by the Japanese.

The end of the journey for the men of the Luzon Force would be Camp O'Donnell, a former temporary Philippine Army post. In March, on orders from General Homma, Colonel Takatsu and Major Wada had made an inspection trip to the camp. They reported that, with the addition of extra buildings and facilities, O'Donnell would be adequate to handle the anticipated number of prisoners. On the basis of this conclusion, the Japanese decided to intern their captives here, and made their plans accordingly.

This, then, was how General Homma intended to evacuate his Filipino and American prisoners from Bataan. In general, his plan conformed to the terms of the Geneva Prisoner of War Convention, a treaty Japan had signed but then refused to ratify. In February, 1942, however, the Japanese had informed the International Red Cross that, while they did not consider themselves bound by the Convention, they would apply it "in so far as possible" to prisoners of war and civilian internees.

Included in General Homma's plan as issued to the 14th Army—perhaps in recognition of the dictates of the Geneva Convention—was an order for unit commanders to treat their captives with a "friendly spirit." Neither the plan nor this order, unfortunately, was carried out as issued.

5

Weaknesses and Miscalculations

Under the best of circumstances, the Japanese plan would have been difficult to execute. The assembly, organization, and movement from Bataan to Camp O'Donnell of thousands of Filipino and American prisoners was a complex and demanding operation. That it proved to be a tragic and horrible episode was due to a number of fatal errors.

First of all, the plan had certain weaknesses, which should have been evident to Homma but which he apparently dismissed or overlooked in his general concern about the coming battle for southern Bataan.

The evacuation of the prisoners had been divided into two phases, yet there was no single officer in over-all command. Colonel Takatsu had the first phase, General Kawane the second. Kawane's was more important, but in many ways dependent on Takatsu's ability to carry out properly his phase of the plan. Yet Kawane evidently had no control over Takatsu.

Thus, Kawane was responsible for moving the prisoners north from Balanga. But it was Takatsu who would organize them for this move, presumably according to his own ideas, which might not necessarily fit in with Kawane's plans.

Kawane would provide any transportation that the captives might be allowed, but any Luzon Force vehicles that could be used for this purpose would have been captured below Balanga, in Takatsu's area. And Takatsu, who also had other responsibilities for which he would need trucks and cars, might not be willing to relinquish them to Kawane, or even to tell him about them.

All the weaknesses of divided military command were inherent in this plan. Yet, taken alone, these might not have been fatal. Close coordination between Kawane and Takatsu, or insistence by General Kawane on the prerogatives of his rank, might have overcome them. But in the final analysis, they were far less important to the final outcome of the evacuation plan than another tragic mistake, one not susceptible of being corrected.

This was the fact that the 14th Army plan was based on three gross miscalculations, and was thus inadequate from the very start.

The first miscalculation was a faulty estimate by the Japanese of the number of prisoners they would take. The 14th Army staff had never had a clear picture of just how many Filipino and American troops were actually on Bataan, and all guesses were consistently low. The first estimate, made just after MacArthur's forces had reached Bataan, set their strength at between 40,000 and 45,000 men. Estimates made during February and March did not change this figure radically, and 14th Army staff officers reckoned the number of expected prisoners at anywhere from 25,000 to at most about twice that number.

The actual number of troops in the Luzon Force was slightly more than 78,000. While General Homma was not aware of this, he was still somewhat skeptical of the low estimates his staff officers were giving him. He nearly lost his temper when Lt. Colonel Hikaru Haba, his intelligence officer, suggested that the Luzon Force strength was down to 25,000 men. "You go back and estimate again," directed Homma. Haba's next attempt raised the figure to 40,000, which Homma still felt was a little low. But without any strong evidence to the contrary, he was forced to accept it. And it was this estimate—40,000 enemy troops—on which the plan to evacuate the prisoners was based.

Even after the fall of Bataan, the Japanese were still ignorant of the size of the Luzon Force. A communiqué issued in Tokyo on April 14th, five days after King's surrender, claimed that 40,000 American and Filipino troops had been captured on Bataan. Given the tendency of Japanese propaganda to exaggerate, this statement further bears out the fact that the 14th Army underestimated the size of King's forces by nearly 50 per cent, an incredible but actual error.

Significantly, even the American War Department did not know until the end of March just how many troops were in the Luzon Force. And strangely enough, when the news of General King's surrender was announced in Washington, the number of American and Filipino soldiers on Bataan was set at 36,853, less than half the actual number.

There is no indication that the Japanese were at all aware of the 26,000 civilians trapped behind the Luzon Force lines. If they were, perhaps they felt no responsibility for them. In any event, no special provisions were made for the care of these unfortunates.

The second miscalculation on which the 14th Army plan for the prisoners was based was probably even more tragic in its consequences than the first. This was a completely erroneous impression of the physical condition of the troops in the Luzon Force.

As early as January 7th, only two days after MacArthur had cut the ration on Bataan, the 14th Army reported that the Bataan. defenders "seem to have reduced their rations by half and take only two meals a day." And in February one Japanese commander noted that the Filipino troops opposing his unit "had apparently suffered considerably from lack of food . . . and came wandering near our front line in search of rice, water-buffaloes, etc."

Yet Homma and his staff had no real knowledge of just how bad the food situation actually was in southern Bataan. Of the prisoners taken by the Japanese during three months of fighting on Bataan, only a handful said they were surrendering because of the shortage of food. And when prisoners captured on different sectors of the front were specifically interrogated about the food, their answers were so varied that Homma's intelligence section could not assess the situation with any certainty. Homma himself reported in March that the Filipino officers were "never allowed to go hungry."

Throughout the campaign, the 14th Army believed that

the Americans and Filipinos had larger stocks of food than they actually did, that supplies continued to slip through the Japanese blockade to some degree, and that Corregidor housed a considerable reserve supply of food, reportedly enough for two years. Indeed, in a message of final instructions to his major unit commanders just before they launched the Good Friday offensive, Homma did not even mention the food situation in the Luzon Force—a surprising oversight if he had any comprehension of how bad it was. He spoke of a lack of discipline and equipment as the defenders' major weaknesses, but apparently did not regard the question of food as sufficiently important to merit discussion.

"We were vaguely aware that [the] food situation in the defense force was not good," declared Homma after the war, "but . . . we judged that [the Luzon Force] could hold out several months longer at least as far as food was concerned." Certainly, he added, had he known that there was only a week's supply of rations left in southern Bataan on April 3rd, he would not have launched an attack in which he expected to take heavy casualties. Instead, he would simply have sat back and waited for an offer of surrender when General King's food ran out.

The toll that disease was taking of the Bataan defenders was also unknown to the Japanese. Southern Bataan was infested with malaria. Indeed, it was one of the most malarial spots in the world. Every American war plan for Bataan had emphasized the necessity of providing adequate supplies of quinine for the troops. Yet these dangers were not readily apparent to the Japanese in the northern half of the peninsula, where malaria was relatively limited. Indeed, it was not until 14th Army troops broke through the Bagac-Orion line in early April that they were fully exposed to the disease.

From December until the end of March, there were about 3,000 cases of malaria in the 14th Army. But in the single month of April, after the Japanese had pushed into southern Bataan, roughly 28,000 of Homma's troops came down with it. One division was reduced to a third of its strength, with the division commander and all of his staff in bed.

Clearly, had General Homma realized the prevalence of malaria in southern Bataan, he would have taken steps to prevent an epidemic among his own troops. That he did nothing along these lines until the sudden frightening increase of malaria in the 14th Army itself is an indication that he never expected such a situation. Nor was he aware of the spread of disease in the Luzon Force.

The third major error on which the Japanese plan for the prisoners was based was a logical result of the second, accentuated somewhat, perhaps, by General Homma's caution. Having been unable to defeat the Bataan defenders during the first three months of 1942, and believing their physical condition to be almost as good as that of his own troops, the Japanese commander was prepared for a long, hard fight. "Man has a tendency to under-rate his enemy," wrote Homma in March and he, for one, did not intend to make this error. He estimated that it would take about a month—to the end of April—to win final victory on Bataan.

On the basis of this estimate, General Kawane, Colonel Takatsu, and their co-planners would have ample time to make arrangements for the reception and movement of the prisoners. None of them was free from his many regular duties in the preparation and execution of the Good Friday offensive, so a few extra weeks in which to get ready for the prisoners were most welcome.

The 20th of April, they believed, would see all arrangements complete. By then, troops to guard and move the captives would have been picked, resting and feeding points designated, rations assembled, and sanitary facilities constructed. Medical units would be ready to care for the sick and wounded, and preparations at Camp O'Donnell would be completed. And all of this would be accomplished ten days before the expected end of the fighting.

The fall of Bataan less than one week after the start of the Good Friday offensive brought the 14th Army face to face with a completely unexpected situation. It was suddenly required to take care of twice the numbers of prisoners expected—a large percentage of them too weak or sick to make the journey out of Bataan on foot—three weeks before it was ready to accommodate even the number and type of captives originally anticipated.

To do this properly would have required resources that General Homma did not have.

In the total scheme of Japanese conquest in the Far East, the Philippine campaign was only a supporting operation for the main drive into Malaya and the Netherlands Indies. The 14th Army, therefore, was assigned a second priority on troops, supplies, and equipment—and suffered accordingly.

The deficiencies with which General Homma was faced were not restricted to shortages of troops and matériel. By the latter part of January, the 14th Army's supply of rice, the most important part of the Japanese ration, had become dangerously low and it was necessary to request more rice from Tokyo. But this request, and others like it, went unanswered. Efforts to procure rice in the Philippines were almost equally unsuccessful.

By the middle of February, General Homma was forced to follow MacArthur's example. He ordered the 14th Army daily ration cut to about one-half of the usual issue.

The normal Japanese field ration consisted of boiled rice, with wheat sometimes mixed into it, pickled plums or radishes, bean soup, vegetables, fish, occasionally meat, and, on special occasions, sweets and fruits. As unappetizing and inadequate as this may appear to the Western palate, it was even worse when cut. The reduced 14th Army ration consisted of about twenty ounces of rice each day, some vegetables now and then, roughly two ounces of canned fish or meat twice a week, and very small amounts of other, minor items.

There was a saying in the Japanese Army that "the samurai displays a toothpick even when he hasn't eaten." The soldier, in other words, should be too proud to admit that he was hungry. Proud or not, front-line Japanese troops on Bataan, like their Luzon Force counterparts, were soon supplementing their meager diet by hunting water buffalo and grubbing for roots. "It was unpleasant," reported one officer, "but starvation was prevented."

The Japanese troop reinforcements that arrived on Luzon in March presumably brought some food supplies with them. Yet these were apparently insufficient to affect the over-all ration situation in the 14th Army.

Japanese forces in the Philippines also suffered from a

shortage of medical supplies, equipment, and personnel. Attempts to alleviate this situation were far from successful, and General Homma's requests to his superiors for medical aid had no more luck than his pleas for rice.

Hospital facilities at the beginning of the Philippine invasion were only half of what the Japanese army normally considered adequate for a force the size of the 14th Army. These facilities were further reduced in January by the loss of field hospitals and medical personnel being transferred from the Philippines to areas with higher priorities. So under strength was the 14th Army medical department on Bataan that wounded Japanese, who might otherwise have been saved, often died in the field before they could be carried back to hospitals.

Medicine was in extremely short supply. Only one month's stock of quinine had been made available to the 14th Army before the start of operations—and this despite the fact that the Philippines were known to be a malaria area. Even mosquito netting and repellent was scarce. General Homma actually had to supplement his quinine supply by buying atabrine, not a standard item of issue in the Japanese army at this time, on the open market in Japan. And he could only purchase a small amount of the drug.

The 14th Army medical officer, Colonel Shusuke Horiguchi, testified after the war that he had only a third as much medicine as he required for the prevention and treatment of gas gangrene and tetanus. For want of emetin, the Japanese doctors prescribed powdered charcoal as a remedy for dysentery. Japan had been importing emetin from Germany via the Soviet Union, but Hitler's invasion of Russia cut off this supply and, complained Horiguchi, the 14th Army was issued only 1 per cent of what he needed. Finally, should diphtheria, always a possibility, strike Japanese troops in the Philippines, Horiguchi had no antitoxin with which to treat it.

In January, finally, Colonel Horiguchi sent a strong request to Tokyo for supplies to alleviate these deficiencies. Describing his grave shortages, he pointed out the obvious difficulty of providing proper medical support for the 14th Army unless he received adequate supplies. The only response that he received to this request was a message stating that "a study" would be made of the situation. But neither the results of this "study" nor any further supplies were sent to him.

The failure of the Japanese high command to provide the 14th Army with additional medical supplies meant a constant decrease in stocks on hand in the Philippines. By mid-January, quinine had become so scarce that it was no longer used as a prophylactic agent except for troops on the front line. The issue of preventive quinine was stopped completely in early March, for only enough remained at that time to treat the seriously ill. Some malaria patients were taking aspirin as a quinine substitute. Shortages of other medicines also left their mark, and the Japanese troops quickly fell prey to dysentery and other diseases prevalent in the tropics.

From January 1st to the end of March, approximately 13,000 cases of disease were reported. With the sick from the month of December and the men wounded in action, this made for a total of nearly 20,000 potential or actual hospital cases. In April the malaria rate shot up nearly tenfold and almost doubled the number of hospital patients.

With only 5,000 beds available to handle patients in 14th Army hospitals, medical facilities were swamped and doctors and staffs overworked. Philippine hospitals in Manila were crowded and poorly equipped, and field hospitals were even worse off. One wounded Japanese soldier wrote in his diary that the field hospital where he was a patient was "just a shack with straw floors, built in tiers on a hill." The larger, so-called "line of communications," hospitals, while somewhat more comfortable, were also terribly overcrowded. Equipped to handle 1,000 patients at the most, they were forced to accommodate five or six times as many. Many other sick or wounded Japanese troops had no better luck than to be treated, in Colonel Horiguchi's words, "in tents by their respective units, in the mountains, under trees or by the rivers."

It is clear that the Japanese supply system left much to be desired, even though conditions in the 14th Army were not as bad as in the Luzon Force. General Homma's forces on Luzon totaled nearly 81,000 men. Feeding these troops and keeping them healthy had become a major problem even before the surrender of General King gave the Japanese the additional task of caring for the men of the Luzon Force. The responsibility suddenly and unexpectedly thrust on Homma for more than 100,000 Filipino and American troops and civilians increased the demand on 14th Army supplies by well over 100 per cent.

The fact that a large percentage of these prisoners were sick and starving only made matters worse.

III
The Assembly at Balanga

6

"Your Worries Are Over"

The first American prisoners to reach Balanga were General King and three of the officers who had surrendered with him. Headquarters of the 14th Army and the chosen assembly point for the captives, the small Filipino town lay hot and dusty under the burning tropical sun. A few trees cast their shadows on its streets, and the Talisay River, its warm waters reduced to a narrow stream in the midst of the dry season, flowed weakly through the parched fields south of the town. Nothing else offered any relief from the scorching heat. The Japanese flag hung limply over the small frame building occupied by the 14th Army staff, while small groups of soldiers busied themselves at various tasks around the headquarters. Along the East Road, which split the town, Japanese supply trucks occasionally moved south.

Otherwise, Balanga was quiet, almost empty. The tens of thousands of Filipino and American prisoners who would soon fill the town and surrounding fields had not yet arrived. The tragic battle for Bataan, its death and destruction now ended, seemed a long way off.

King and his party arrived on the afternoon of April 9th. No sooner had they climbed out of their jeeps than they were subjected to the attentions of Japanese military and civilian photographers. After nearly an hour of picture taking, the four Americans were questioned at length by a 14th Army staff officer. The Japanese officer was interested in many things, but mainly in the defenses of Corregidor.

To all questions about operations on Bataan, the size of the Luzon Force, and his supply situation, King answered freely. But he refused, firmly yet politely, to give any information about Corregidor. The Japanese asked about the artillery on the island fortress. How many guns were there, and how were they emplaced? King disclaimed any knowledge of this. What about the troops on Corregidor? What sort of positions did they occupy, and in what strength? Again King pleaded ignorance. When the Japanese pressed him, he simply declined to answer any further questions about Corregidor.

But there was one more. The 14th Army staff had heard of Malinta Tunnel, a huge underground labyrinth dug into a hill on Corregidor, the site of General Wainwright's headquarters and the island's hospital. For some reason, the Japanese assumed that this was a tunnel from Bataan to Corregidor, and King's interrogator pressed him on this point. The American commander could hardly keep from laughing. There was no tunnel between Bataan and Corregidor, and it was some time before he could convince the Japanese of this point. Late in the afternoon, finally, the interrogation came to an abrupt halt. The Americans were left once again to the attentions of the cameramen.

About an hour later, a Japanese colonel approached the four prisoners and introduced himself in broken English. His name sounded like Takasaki, but Japanese records show no Colonel Takasaki on Bataan at this time and he may actually have been Colonel Takatsu, the officer in charge of assembling the Luzon Force troops at Balanga. At any rate, he ordered some food for King and his companions, their first meal of the day. It was an odd but welcome repast: hot condensed milk and warm beer. Then the colonel sat down and began to talk.

"Ah, now for you the war is over," he said, "and so now we are all friends."

"Yes, for us the war is over," nodded King politely, "but we are not friends; we are your prisoners."

"Oh, no," insisted the Japanese, "we are friends."

At any rate, the colonel seemed to think so, for that evening he entertained the four Americans as guests at his quarters, a large house in Orani, eight miles to the north. Here King and the others enjoyed the luxury of a bath and ate a large and excellent chicken dinner. But the end of the evening was somewhat less satisfying. After eating, they were taken to a small, filthy storeroom in the center of town where they slept on the floor that night.

The four Americans remained in Orani until April 12th. They spent much of that time undergoing further interrogation and greeting other high ranking officers of the Luzon Force as they arrived at Orani. Treatment here was good, and the food adequate. On the evening of the 12th, after another session with the cameramen, King and General Jones, the I Corps commander, along with two Filipino generals, were packed tightly into a car and taken to Camp O'Donnell. They were the first prisoners to arrive there. Not once had King seen General Homma, nor was he ever to meet the Japanese commander.

Of the group that had gone forward with General King on the morning of the 9th, only Colonel Collier and Major Hurt had been allowed to return to the Luzon Force lines. Accompanied by a Japanese officer, they had been sent back to pass the news of the surrender to Brigadier General Arnold J. Funk, King's chief of staff, and to Generals Parker and Jones, the corps commanders.

The three men set out in an American jeep immediately after the surrender. Before long they began to meet small groups of Filipino soldiers. These they sent on their way toward the East Road. Above the town of Cabcaben, at the southeast corner of Bataan, they encountered a force of Japanese tanks that had stopped and trained their guns on what was left of a battalion of Philippine Constabulary troops. The Filipinos were dug in about 150 yards away and obviously had no intention of giving up. Between the two forces stood the Filipino commander, a small major, with his pistol but four feet from the stomach of the Japanese tank commander.

Turning to Collier, the major exclaimed in a voice trembling with emotion, "Colonel, this SOB demands my surrender and I am not going to surrender and if he makes a move to give a command I'm going to shoot him in two."

"I shall always feel," recalled Colonel Collier, "that the tank commander would have been permanently relieved from his command and other worldly duties within the next five or ten minutes but, I fear, so would the major and some two hundred of his men." To avert this disaster, Collier stepped between the two men, told the Filipino of General King's surrender, and disarmed him. The situation had been saved, but Collier knew that he would have to work fast to spread the word of the surrender if he was to prevent similar occurrences elsewhere.

Leaving the Constabulary troops to the Japanese tank unit, he and the others pushed on to the vicinity of Cabcaben where the last II Corps line of resistance had been tentatively established. Collier and Hurt told the troops along this line about the surrender and they, in turn, agreed to pass the word along.

The two Americans and their Japanese escort now started for Luzon Force headquarters to see General Funk. Hardly had they gone a short distance, however, when they met a column of Japanese infantry circling to take the Cabcaben line from the rear. The Japanese officer succeeded in halting the column, but he had to go all the way back to General Nagano's headquarters for written orders before he could persuade the infantry commander to call off his attack.

By now it was five o'clock. Collier and the others started south again, only to be halted once more, this time by an imposing traffic jam. As far as the eye could see, both lanes of the road were packed solidly with vehicles of all description and civilian and military pedestrians, the latter carrying white flags. It was impossible to go any further by jeep. As they climbed out and began to walk, a soldier from Luzon Force headquarters informed Collier that General Funk had already learned of the surrender and that Funk, in turn, had notified General Jones. It was evident to Collier that he had now done all he could. The two Americans and their escort got back into their jeep and returned to Japanese lines.

In a mango grove about a mile north of the point where General King had surrendered, the Japanese officer stopped the jeep. This was the 14th Army forward command post on Bataan. Leaving Major Hurt alone, the Japanese took Collier forward to meet a tall, heavy-set officer whom he described as "the commanding general." To Collier's surprise, he soon learned that he was in the presence of General Homma.

Colonel Collier was the only American officer to meet the Japanese commander. For about forty minutes, he recalls, he and Homma "had a pleasant conversation." The two sat on folding chairs by a small table and talked informally without an interpreter, since Homma spoke English. Relaxed and friendly, the 14th Army commander asked a number of questions about the fighting on Luzon and then boasted that he would "have Corregidor within a week"—a curious statement in view of his earlier pessimism about the Good Friday offensive.

When Colonel Collier said he would like to rejoin General King, Homma dictated a short order, signed it, and gave it to the American to use as a pass. "Your worries are over," he said as he bade Collier goodbye. "Japan treats her prisoners well. You may even see Japan in cherry blossom time and that is a beautiful sight."

Meanwhile the officers at Luzon Force headquarters had waited anxiously most of the day for news of the outcome of the surrender negotiations. In accordance with King's orders, almost all shooting had ceased about dawn. By afternoon, for the first time since the beginning of the year, the noise of battle could no longer be heard on Bataan. "All firing has died down," noted one officer in his diary. "The quiet is strange."

Toward evening, a group of Japanese tanks pushed its way into the headquarters area and the tank commander informed the Americans that King had surrendered. The Japanese allowed the men to spend the night where they were but, after breakfast on the morning of the 10th, Funk and the others were ordered into their own vehicles for a trip to General Hospital No. 1, a few miles to the west.

The short trip to the hospital over the crowded Bataan trails took quite a while. For the first time, General Funk and his men could see the disorganized state of the Luzon Force units and the confused efforts of the Japanese troops attempting to round them up. "Traffic was uncontrolled," wrote one officer later, "termite-like, and in extraordinary congestion; with Filipino refugees moving out under enemy direction, prodding, and organized stripping; and enemy troops of all categories moving in." So confused was the situation that the group from Luzon Force headquarters was stopped and turned around on the trail three separate times on the orders of different staff officers and interpreters.

At General Hospital No. 1, the Japanese assembled about a dozen officers from King's headquarters. Like General King, these officers were questioned at length about Corregidor's defenses and about the supposed Bataan-Corregidor tunnel. Like King, again, they failed to give their captors any satisfaction. Finally, at about five in the afternoon, Funk and his men were again ordered into their cars and this time told to drive to Balanga. Some of them moved under Japanese guard, others alone. Those driving on their own were frequently stopped by traffic jams or by Japanese soldiers who searched them and took what they pleased. The others, protected by their guards, were spared such interruptions. Brigadier General James R. N. Weaver, the American tank commander on Bataan, was told to drive his own car all the way to Camp O'Donnell. Surprisingly enough, he made it.

With some exceptions, most of the Americans in Funk's group had thus far received "very courteous treatment," as one of them put it later. At Balanga, however, there was a change. Here the Japanese searched them thoroughly and relieved them of all razors, flashlights, cameras, scissors, nail files, and, depending on the searcher, some money. This process was completed shortly after midnight. Then the Americans were counted, assigned to sedans or trucks, and driven north to Camp O'Donnell.

"The road by this time was deserted," recalled one officer, "and the weather clear with brilliant stars overhead. Had our ride been under different conditions, it would have been a pleasure."

7

I and II Corps Give Up

As word of General King's impending surrender reached the rear areas on the morning of April 9th, the scattered, disorganized units of the Luzon Force began preparing to receive their Japanese conquerors. The troops hoisted white flags on the tops of hills and in other prominent places, stacked arms or destroyed their weapons and ammunition, and made large piles of whatever other equipment was still left. At the Mariveles and Cabcaben airstrips, large crowds assembled under white flags.

At Mariveles, the men spread sheets on the ground and made huge "rising sun" flags by painting them with Mercurochrome. Suddenly Japanese planes swooped down, their machine guns wide open, killing or wounding many men. Another air attack struck Cabcaben. Then the planes departed. The weary, hungry, dirty, unshaven troops lay on the ground to rest and wait. Under trees and bushes to avoid the sun's punishing rays, some tried to sleep. Others stared blankly ahead, remembering the past or attempting to pierce the obscurity of the future.

On the afternoon of the 8th, General Wainwright had directed the 45th Infantry Regiment—Philippine Scouts led by American officers—to try to make it to Mariveles, where barges were waiting to withdraw the unit to Corregidor. Unfortunately, the men could not reach Mariveles soon enough, and few if any of them escaped. At the time of the surrender, Captain Paul H. Krauss, commanding the regimental antitank company, was attempting to move his unit down the traffic-snarled West Road through a confused jam of men and vehicles. It was soon obvious to him that he was getting nowhere, and he decided to report to Brigadier General Maxon S. Lough, his divisional commander, for new orders. When he reached the Philippine Division command post, Lough told him that General King had given up. "Do we have to surrender?" asked Krauss. Lough replied that they did. In the fluid situation on Bataan, it might be possible for many men to slip through the Japanese lines and hide out in central Luzon. But, he explained, if there was any large-scale escape, the Japanese might make hostages of the troops that did surrender, with dire consequences for the prisoners. So any attempt to escape would be regarded as desertion. But Krauss should not worry, added Lough. He was sure that the Japanese would abide by the Geneva Convention and treat their prisoners properly.

Meanwhile, Japanese troops—infantrymen of the 4th Division—had reached General Parker's II Corps headquarters on the morning of the 9th. Although King had not yet surrendered at this time, the Japanese seemed to know that the end had come and were more intent on looting than fighting.

A few of them had just entered the command post kitchen area when Lieutenant Colonel John H. Ball, the corps artillery officer, discovered them. The Japanese soldiers were clad in dusty khaki uniforms and carried light combat packs. At the front of their small woolen field caps, each wore a gold star: the symbol of the Japanese army. Their necks were shielded from the sun by a flap of cloth that hung from the rear of the cap—similar to that on a French legionnaire's hat—and the spiral wool puttees wrapped around their legs resembled those worn by American troops in World War I. There was no mistaking the meaning of the rifle and fixed bayonet that each man carried.

Ball raised his hands in surrender and one of the Japanese immediately made a grab for the fountain pen in the colonel's shirt pocket. When Ball pointed to his insignia of rank in hopes of saving the pen, the Japanese hauled off and struck him a blow in the stomach. "He got the fountain pen," recalled Ball.

Other Japanese, tank troops as well as infantry, quickly moved into the area. They searched each American or Filipino and took whatever struck their fancy. There seemed to be no order or control of any kind. If one of the prisoners hesitated or refused to give up his possessions, he was beaten and robbed anyway.

Finally, at General Parker's request, Colonel Gempachi Sato, the local Japanese infantry commander, posted a guard to protect the II Corps commander and his immediate staff.

Sato also personally returned much of the stolen property to Parker. The men huddled together behind their Japanese guard, worried, apprehensive, and uncertain.

A few days later, General Parker was driven to Camp O'Donnell. The rest of the two to three hundred American and Filipino troops in the area were less fortunate. Without either information or food from the Japanese, they were left to speculate on their fate and to care for themselves as best they could. The Japanese allowed them to form details to get water for drinking and cooking, and to eat whatever meager provisions they still had.

Not until a week after the surrender, still ignorant of what the future might hold, did they begin to move to Balanga. Some of the sick were placed on two old trucks with the baggage. The rest of the men walked.

Almost all of the other II Corps troops had already started for Balanga. These men had laid down their arms on April 9th, and most were in Japanese custody by the 10th at the latest. The surrender had been a confused affair, since few of the Filipino and American soldiers were still in organized units on the 9th. Great masses of men were spread across the jungled hills of southeastern Bataan, streaming to the rear in disorganized groups, clogging the trails in growing confusion. As word of the surrender spread, many of the men just sat down where they were to await the Japanese. Others were soon overtaken or cut off by Japanese units that knifed their way through the area in growing numbers.

In one instance, Japanese troops advanced with fixed bayonets on a small group of Americans waiting to surrender. The Japanese gave no indication that they knew the fighting was over and Sergeant Spud Murphy, the ranking noncom, shouted to one of his men to stand up and wave the white flag they had prepared. But the soldier, too frightened to do anything, was lying flat on the ground. "If you want this white flag waved," he yelled, "come on and wave it yourself." With a burst of profanity, Murphy ran quickly over to the man, grabbed the flag, and swung it back and forth over his head. Only then did the Japanese lower their rifles. The officer in command, who spoke some English, told Murphy that he was under orders to advance further south. He directed the Americans to head for the East Road on their own, but warned them to keep waving their white flag.

The only large II Corps force that still retained some organization on April 9th consisted of about 1,300 Americans and Philippine Scouts under Brigadier General Clifford Bluemel, trying to form a line northeast of Cabcaben. Informed by Colonel Collier of the surrender, many of these men threw down their weapons and began to hoist white flags. Most of the exhausted and hungry soldiers would hardly have been able to continue the struggle anyway. The veteran Scouts in Captain Fred Yeager's rifle company, for example, were all well-disciplined soldiers and good fighters, but they had gone for two days without food and could barely stay on their feet. Other units were no better off. Nevertheless, General Bluemel wanted to keep on fighting. But as more and more white flags went up along the line, he realized the futility of it all. For two days the tough little general had commanded the only units still opposing the Japanese advance. Now, utterly worn out, he flung his rifle on the ground in disgust and sat down to await his conquerors.

A few American officers considered taking off to the hills in an attempt to make their way north out of Bataan. But they were unwilling to desert their Filipino enlisted men, and quickly abandoned the idea. Major Allan M. Cory, for example, elected to stay with his unit. "I was a battalion commander," he explained recently, "and until I was relieved I had a responsibility to stay there." But when one of his officers, an American captain, asked permission to try to escape, Cory saw no reason to forbid it. "You know the risks," said Cory as he wished him well. With two Filipino companions, the captain made his way to the coast, stole a small banca, and managed to sail all the way to southern Luzon. Eventually, he made it safely to Australia.

Another American officer, Major James C. Blanning, solved the problem of his responsibility to his men without any difficulty. In command of a troop of about thirty Scouts of the 26th Cavalry, Blanning gave the Filipinos their choice of yielding to the Japanese or of trying to escape. The tough veterans did not hesitate. They preferred to take their chances in the mountains and, with Blanning's approval, swiftly melted into the jungle.

But most of the men had no time even to think of escaping before they were surrounded by Japanese units who closed in still firing their weapons. At Bluemel's direction, Colonel Lee C. Vance, the 26th Cavalry commander, went out to meet the Japanese with a white flag. The Japanese soldiers ceased firing, but one private immediately grabbed Vance and stripped him of all his equipment and personal possessions. Soon the Japanese were all over the area, looting the men of watches, rings, and other items. One Japanese who was searching Captain Yeager pointed to his West Point class ring and indicated that he wanted it. When Yeager refused to give it up, the Japanese drew his pistol. Another American officer standing nearby said, "Give it to him, Fred. It isn't worth it." Yeager suddenly came to his senses and gave the Japanese his ring. All he had left now was his toothbrush, handkerchief, and canteen.

A Japanese lieutenant grabbed General Bluemel's pistol and threw it on the ground, then shoved him roughly over to another officer. This one had a map and, while a third Japanese kept his pistol trained on Bluemel, he questioned him about his position and operations.

Soon all the prisoners were divided into two groups, Americans in one and Filipinos in the other. With Bluemel at their head, and the Japanese all around them, they began to march toward the East Road. After about two or three hours, the column halted at an abandoned Filipino barrio. It was now dusk and the Japanese indicated that the prisoners would spend the night here. They gave their captives no food or water, but the Filipinos and Americans were so exhausted that they quickly fell asleep.

This luxury was denied Bluemel. With Colonel Vance and the three next ranking officers, he was forced to march for another hour and one-half until the five men reached General Nagano's headquarters. Here a Japanese officer questioned them about their operations on Bataan, but the Americans were so exhausted they could barely answer him. Lieutenant Colonel Pete Calyer could not stay awake and slumped forward asleep. The Japanese officer struck him rudely across the back with his riding crop and Calyer snapped up. Thereafter he forced himself to stay awake. The Japanese also hit Bluemel with a sheaf of papers when he thought the American general was lying to him.

After spending about a day at Nagano's headquarters, the five officers were turned over to another Japanese detachment near Cabcaben. By now Corregidor had begun to return the fire of Japanese artillery pieces on Bataan, and a Japanese officer told Bluemel that he and the others would be held in the zone of the Corregidor shellfire until the island surrendered. But on the 15th the five Americans were placed on a truck and taken to Balanga.

In western Bataan, meanwhile, the men of the I Corps had retained their liberty for a day or two longer than had their comrades to the east. The Japanese had made only a diversionary attack on General Jones' corps during the Good Friday offensive and on April 9th the defenders were in positions just a few miles below the line they had held a week earlier. While hungry and worn out, they had suffered far fewer casualties and were much better organized than the men of the II Corps.

Word of General King's surrender reached Jones late on the afternoon of the 9th, and he in turn passed the news on to his subordinate commanders. Most of them had the information by evening and began to stack arms and make other preparations to receive the Japanese. As night fell, the troops lit great fires so that their white flags of surrender could be clearly seen in the dark. Some men seized the opportunity to get a good night's sleep—their first in weeks—and in the morning bathed and put on fresh clothes in which to await the Japanese. A few I Corps units did not get definite word of the surrender until the morning of the 10th, when they too made ready to give up.

Toward evening on the 9th, large numbers of fleeing men from the II Corps began coming west into the rear of the I Corps positions. A few hours later, as dusk began to settle, pursuing troops of the Japanese 65th Brigade crashed into the exposed right flank of the I Corps. Apparently expecting to meet resistance, they advanced in combat formation, firing their weapons.

As the defenders fell back in confusion before the Japanese infantry and tanks, General Jones found himself in a dilemma. He wanted to surrender his corps in accordance with his orders. But this would be most difficult and dangerous to attempt if the Japanese were unwilling to let him. All he could do was to order his right flank units to hold the Japanese as long as possible until a surrender could be arranged.

In the rear of the corps area, men in one American unit could hear the sounds of explosions and machine gun fire. Their nerves on edge over the possibility that the Japanese might not accept the surrender, they were further upset by the rumors that floated back to them. "We heard," wrote one man in his diary, "that all Americans were to report to a certain spot for surrender and that in just that spot it sounded like they were bombing and machine gunning. It really put the fear of the devil in all of us. A number of the boys broke down under the strain."

Not everyone panicked, though. On the corps' right flank, one of the units hit by the attacking 65th Brigade was the 11th Philippine Army Division. Major Russell W. Volckmann and Captain Donald D. Blackburn, two American staff officers in division headquarters, had already made up their minds to take a chance on escaping rather than trust to the uncertain mercies of Japanese captivity. Without food or medicine, it would be difficult to exist for long, but the two men determined to get away. Luck would be with them, they hoped. When the sounds of battle approached the division command post, they knew the time had come to make their break. "This is when!" shouted Volckmann. Blackburn agreed. "Let's get the hell out of here!"

The two officers slipped into a dry stream bed and crawled away from the area. By morning they had made good their escape, and for the next few days avoided Japanese units as they cautiously picked their way north through the jungle mountains. By the time they had left Bataan and reached the relative safety of central Luzon, they had run into dozens of other American and Filipino escapees, some of whom joined forces with them. "It began to look," recalled Volckmann several years later, "as though the mountains and jungles were teeming with Americans."

Back on Bataan, meanwhile, the Japanese facing the left of the I Corps front were apparently informed of General King's surrender almost immediately. Instead of attacking, they advanced slowly into the western half of the corps position and took the surrender of each unit they encountered.

Below Bagac on the evening of the 9th, Colonel Virgil N. Cordero was checking his unit, the 72nd Infantry, when suddenly he heard small arms fire coming from one front-line position. He rushed forward and discovered that an ammunition truck was ablaze and that .30-caliber rifle rounds were exploding in all directions. Realizing that the Japanese might mistake the shooting for an attack, Cordero immediately set about putting out the fire. With no thought for his own safety, he ignored the exploding ammunition and soon had the blaze under control. For this act of bravery, he was subsequently decorated with the Silver Star, the Army's third highest decoration.

The Japanese were accepting the surrender of more and more units in western Bataan. They treated the prisoners courteously, without any violence, usually leaving them alone once each unit had given up. They simply ordered the Filipinos and Americans to move either north to Bagac or south to Mariveles. Most of the captured men made the trip unguarded.

One American stopped by Japanese troops below Bagac was Captain Krauss, the 45th Infantry antitank company commander. While still at division headquarters, he had received word to report to General Jones. Jones, it seemed, had only one aide assigned to him, although he was entitled to two. Thinking that a general's aide might fare better than an ordinary prisoner in Japanese hands, Jones had directed that a deserving infantry officer be assigned as his other aide. The choice fell on Krauss. Turning his company over to a Filipino lieutenant, Krauss had started toward I Corps headquarters late on the 10th. As he and his driver moved up the West Road that evening, they suddenly came on a group of Japanese preparing to halt for the night. The Japanese refused to let them pass, so the two men lay down to sleep beside their jeep.

In the morning, while the Japanese were preparing their

breakfast, Krauss indicated by sign language that he wanted to continue. He was getting nowhere until finally a Japanese who spoke some English approached. Krauss addressed him boldly, stating in a self-assured and commanding fashion that it was absolutely essential that he go on to meet General Jones. Had he known then what he learned later about the Japanese soldiers, Krauss observed recently, he would not have dared to act so assertively. But now his bluff worked, for the Japanese finally agreed to let him go on. Curiously, they made no move to disarm him, but they did want to siphon some gasoline from his jeep. Fortunately for Krauss, the jeep's ignition was turned off, so the needle in the gas gauge rested on "empty." Krauss pointed to this as proof that he had no gas to spare, and the Japanese allowed him to proceed without further difficulty. At his insistence, they even wrote him a pass to show to any other Japanese he might encounter.

All this while, General Jones had been waiting to surrender. Just before dark on the evening of the 10th, a Japanese officer from Bagac reached I Corps headquarters. Jones and his men were to sit tight, he said. The Japanese would take his surrender in the morning.

Sometime after sunrise on the 11th, the enemy officer returned. General Jones surrendered those of his troops not already in Japanese hands and he himself became a prisoner.

The general, his chief of staff, and his two aides—Captain Krauss had just arrived—were driven south to Mariveles. On their way down the West Road, they passed a column of Japanese troops who shouted angrily at them and waved their fists. Once, when they had to stop, a Japanese officer put his arm through the open car window and tried to choke Jones.

At Mariveles, finally, the Americans found themselves taking part in a Japanese radio show. A microphone had been set up in a cleared area and the four officers were hauled in front of it. "We were like a few strange animals in a zoo, like pandas," recalled Krauss, "because all of the Japanese officers in camp were surrounding us and just gaped at us."

An interpreter arrived and the Japanese began to question General Jones. After some preliminary sparring with a Japanese staff officer, Jones found himself face to face with Lieutenant General Susumu Morioka, the enemy commander who had opposed him during most of the fighting. A short, thick-set man, Morioka sat on a camp stool, fanning himself in the heat, and spoke politely to Jones. The two men discussed the campaign, Morioka dignified and condescending, Jones proud and unabashed.

"Certainly," asked Morioka, "you Americans don't expect to win this war?"

"We certainly do," responded Jones quickly. "You can't win!"

"Well, *you're* not going to fight anymore."

"No," Jones agreed, "but I have four sons who will be fighting."

When the interview was ended, the Japanese drove Jones and the others to Balanga. After a brief rest, the four Americans were suddenly ordered to join a column of prisoners walking north. Jones was placed at the head of the line of march, with a Japanese guard on a bicycle setting the pace ahead of him. In the heat of the day, with sick and exhausted men behind him, Jones tried to walk as slowly as possible. But each time he slowed his pace, the Japanese on the bicycle rode back and ordered him to hurry. And when he walked a little faster, the men behind him screamed out in protest. Years later, General Jones could still remember their cries. "For God's sake, slow down! We can't keep up!"

As the column moved north, the hot, thirsty men filled their canteens with the stagnant water that had collected in craters along the road. Everyone knew the water was contaminated, but almost all of them drank it, and no one seemed to care. "They just had to have a drink," recalled Jones.

Occasionally trucks loaded with Japanese soldiers headed south would pass. Some of the soldiers had long bamboo poles with which they tried to hit the captives as they went by. The white stars on Jones' shoulders made him a particularly attractive target but Jones, who was short, was able to duck and escape any punishment.

From time to time, the column would halt. Then the Japanese would force the men to squat close together in as small a space as possible. Sometimes passing Japanese soldiers would stop and relieve the prisoners of rings, watches, and other personal property. A Japanese soldier took something from Lieutenant Pete Perkins, General Jones' other aide, and, when Perkins tried to snatch it back, struck him in the face several times. After that, none of the others resisted. An English-speaking Japanese officer was present at one of the halts. "Why are you doing this to us?" asked Jones. "To teach you humility," replied the Japanese.

On another occasion, a Japanese two-star private approached Jones. Pointing to the two stars on Jones' shoulder and to his own similar insignia, he smiled and indicated in sign language that he and the American general had the same rank. Jones smiled back and the two men joked back and forth in sign language. Then the Japanese noticed Jones' watch and made a grab for it. Jones, seeing that the private already had a watch, seized his wrist and indicated that they should trade watches. To the amazement of the watching Americans, who expected to see Jones knocked off his feet, the Japanese nodded in agreement and the transaction was quickly completed.

That evening the column reached Orani. The exhausted prisoners were placed in a crowded barbed-wire enclosure, and Jones and his chief of staff found themselves sitting next to an open-trench latrine. Hungry, completely worn out, and nauseated by the overpowering stench, they passed the night with little sleep. In the morning they were taken out of the enclosure and led to a small house where they met General King. Here, for the first time in twenty-four hours, they were given something to eat.

Around noon, the Japanese took the entire group outside to be photographed. One of the cameramen told General Jones to remove his sunglasses but Jones, who by now had had enough, absolutely refused. Again his companions expected to see him punished, but again Jones' boldness paid off. His sunglasses remained on. Later that afternoon the Japanese began moving the American generals by car to Camp O'Donnell.

Within a few days, most of the other top commanders of the Luzon Force had reached O'Donnell. For them, the movement from Bataan had been relatively easy. Unfortunately, the same was not true for the bulk of the Filipino and American troops who surrendered with them.

8

Surrender at the Hospitals

When General King made his decision to surrender, an important factor in his thinking was the hope that he would be able to halt the Japanese attack before it reached the two Luzon Force general hospitals with their thousands of helpless patients. These hospitals, between Cabcaben and Mariveles on the East Road, lay directly in the path of the Japanese advance. Should 14th Army assault units overrun them before the cease-fire, there was no telling what might happen.

King's decision had come just in time, for on the morning of the 9th, even as he himself was going forward for his meeting with Colonel Nakayama, Japanese tanks reached General Hospital No. 1.

The medical officers at the hospital had been expecting them. All nurses had been evacuated to Corregidor the night before, a huge white bedsheet had replaced the Red Cross flag atop the buildings, and now the ranking officers stood outside to greet the Japanese.

The tank commander's first concern was for a number of wounded Japanese prisoners who were patients in the hospital. There were forty-two of these Japanese wounded, and those who could walk were brought out for his inspection. After much bowing, saluting, and questioning, the tank officer began to relax. His countrymen had been well treated, and this pleased him. So satisfied was he with what he found that he informed the hospital staff that they would be treated with consideration. No one, he said, would bother them or interfere with their work.

The Japanese officer was as good as his word. The 14th Army plan for the prisoners had provided that hospital patients would not be moved immediately. In the case of the 3,000 sick and wounded at General Hospital No. 1, this plan was followed without incident.

There was only one unfortunate event to mar this record —and it was probably beyond the power of the tank commander to prevent it. On April 10th, a number of ambulatory patients, out for an airing, chanced to wander near the main road just as a column of prisoners walked by. Still dressed in their pajamas and slippers, some of them barely able to walk, the unfortunate patients were seen by the Japanese guards and forced to join the moving line of captives. Many were unable to keep up with the column and soon fell by the wayside.

For two and one-half months after King's surrender, the Japanese allowed the staff of General Hospital No. 1 to carry on the work of caring for the sick and wounded there. Treatment was generally good, and most of the time the doctors and their patients were left to themselves.

The Japanese apparently furnished a small but welcome amount of rice to the hospital mess, which was kept supplied in a variety of ways. Those who were able were permitted to forage for wild fruits and vegetables, and one intrepid medical officer actually went hunting for carabao with a Japanese soldier, the first of many daily expeditions. Before long permission was obtained from the Japanese to buy carabao from the natives, who had by now returned to Bataan. This made it possible to serve small portions of meat twice a day, a comparative luxury. No one grew fat, but the diet was adequate. In mid-May, however, food became scarcer, as did the supply of medicine. Finally at the end of June, apparently before these deficiencies grew too bad, the entire hospital was transferred by truck to Camp O'Donnell.

Treatment at General Hospital No. 1 had been good. It was the opposite at Hospital No. 2.

Hospital No. 2 held more than 7,000 sick and wounded, most of them Filipinos. The hospital was not in a building, but consisted simply of a large number of open-air wards and surgical areas stretching for about a mile under the trees beside the road. On the morning of April 9th, as the tide of battle swept south, it was clear to everyone at the hospital that the Japanese could not be far off. The doctors and patients spent most of their time in foxholes and dugouts, seeking shelter from bomb fragments and machine gun bullets that were falling into the area. When word of the surrender reached the hospital in mid-afternoon, Colonel James O. Gillespie, the commanding officer, immediately ordered all available Red Cross flags to be displayed along with two large white bedsheets.

The first Japanese to reach the hospital, a small group of infantry, arrived at about five. They asked for water and then went on. Three hours later, two Japanese officers and half a platoon of riflemen walked into the hospital headquarters and called for the commanding officer.

The leader of this force was Major Sekiguchi, the medical officer who had worked on the plan for evacuating the prisoners from Bataan. From the start, he was stiff and harsh. He announced that he was taking over "from a medical standpoint," and issued peremptory orders for the administration of the hospital. Everyone at the hospital, he asserted, was a prisoner of war, subject to all Japanese rules and regulations. Disobedience meant death. A strict blackout would be maintained and no one would leave the hospital boundaries. All hospital property was under the control of the Japanese Army, which could requisition any item it desired. Sekiguchi then posted a guard throughout the hospital area and gave the ward doctors a password to use when necessary.

When the Japanese officer had finished issuing his orders, Colonel Gillespie asked politely if more food might not be obtained for his hungry patients. Sekiguchi turned him down unsympathetically. He declared, as Lieutenant Colonel Willard H. Waterous recalled it, "that our food would not be increased; it would be decreased if anything. He stated that our forces had not fed us adequately, and that he did not choose to feed us any more than we had been receiving." Besides, said Sekiguchi, all available transportation was needed to support the siege of Corregidor. To the bitterness of the Americans, however, a truckload of food arrived daily for the Japanese.

For several days after the surrender, hundreds of Japanese combat troops passed through the area. They walked into the wards, messes, operating rooms, and supply areas and collected watches, rings, sunglasses, and food. They seemed particularly fond of the limited supply of fruit juices and milk in the hospital, and had a special preference for the few cases of sardines that the cooks had managed to retain. They also helped themselves to precious medicine. The sentries posted by Sekiguchi throughout the area were apparently not intended to protect the staff and patients, for when Japanese soldiers stole from the prisoners, the guards joined in the looting. Many important hospital records were destroyed in the course of the general plundering.

Japanese mechanics found the hospital generators a ready source of supply for replacement parts for their own equipment. In short order, the hospital electrical system broke down. Vehicles and other motor pool supplies were also confiscated and, despite Colonel Gillespie's protests, the Japanese removed enlisted medical technicians from the hospital and set them to work driving and servicing the vehicles.

To all complaints Sekiguchi turned a deaf ear. All property in the area, he reiterated, belonged to the Japanese, and if anything was refused them, the punishment would be severe. No food, he said, would be taken. When Colonel Gillespie protested that Japanese officers had already supervised the removal of a number of truckloads of food, Sekiguchi replied that a receipt would have been given if such had been the case. Since Gillespie could not show him a receipt, it was quite obvious, he said, that the Japanese army had not taken the food. "The Japanese Army is honorable," shouted Sekiguchi angrily, and if Gillespie knew what was good for him he would not raise the subject again.

To the horror of the American doctors, the Japanese troops ignored the basic rules of sanitation. They apparently regarded the entire hospital area as one huge latrine, and used it accordingly. Since many of the Japanese were infected with intestinal diseases, the dangers of contamination were extreme.

Many of the Japanese sick were placed in the wards of the hospital and Major Sekiguchi directed the American doctors to care for them. These Japanese were suffering from malaria and dysentery, and treating them meant a further drain on the hospital's slim resources. Sekiguchi was either unwilling or, more likely, unable, to provide any medication for his countrymen.

On the morning of April 10th, all Filipino doctors and dentists and a small detachment of Philippine Scouts on duty at the hospital were ordered to begin marching north out of Bataan. As they left, word spread among the approximately 5,400 Filipino patients that the sick and wounded men were now free to return to their homes. According to the rumor, the Japanese were releasing all Filipino prisoners. The large numbers of Filipino civilians who passed through the hospital area on their way north seemed to lend credence to this story, and the patients began to depart.

Many believed that Major Sekiguchi had ordered them to leave. This was not so. But as the rumors of freedom spread and the sick and wounded men started toward the road, their belief that they were free and their hasty departure were encouraged by the Japanese guards. Some of these guards even directed the patients to leave.

By evening a long line of Filipinos could be seen trudging from the hospital area. Some, convalescents, were not too badly off, but only half were considered by their American doctors to be truly ambulatory patients. Large numbers were suffering from dysentery, malaria, diarrhea, or malnutrition. Many had only recently been operated on and were still wearing casts or dressings. Some had undergone amputations or serious abdominal surgery. In many cases, the Japanese soldiers ordered patients to remove their casts, or sometimes the Japanese even tore them off themselves. Only about 500 Filipino patients, so weak they could not rise from their beds, were unable to leave. The others, obsessed with the belief that they were free to go home, refused to stay.

"I remember going from ward to ward," recalls Colonel Jack W. Schwartz, then chief surgeon of the hospital, "pleading with Filipino patients who were in no condition to leave the hospital to remain, but my pleas were in vain in most instances."

As the patients left the hospital, they joined the long columns of prisoners moving out of southern Bataan. Some hobbled forward pathetically on makeshift crutches fashioned of tree limbs. Others staggered along, clutching at their wounds to keep the fast loosening dressings from falling off. Only a few carried food or water. Soon the weaker ones began to fall by the roadside, many to be shot or bayoneted to death by the Japanese guards. "Crippled Filipinos were strewn along the road," wrote an American officer who passed by on his way to Balanga, "crawling, creeping, limping—north!"

For those remaining at General Hospital No. 2, life was not easy either. In the days immediately following the surrender, the Japanese had rushed forward their artillery to positions from which they could fire on Corregidor. General Hospital No. 2 was situated in a valley, between two ridges that would afford ample protection for any guns emplaced there. On the 10th then, in complete disregard for the safety of the patients, the Japanese proceeded to ring the hospital with artillery. Colonel Gillespie strongly protested that the remaining patients and doctors should be evacuated, but to no avail. Instead, the Japanese opened fire on Corregidor. A visiting Japanese officer who spoke English was talking with Gillespie when this happened. "Why don't they surrender over there?" he asked. "Many of those poor fellows are dying. All we want is peace."

Corregidor did not return the fire for several days. When it did, the American gunners took great care not to hit the hospital, but shell fragments were still a menace to the doctors and patients. Fortunately the hospital was protected by a dense growth of bamboo clumps and very tall trees. Thanks to these and the availability of dugouts and foxholes, there were few injuries. Shells occasionally burst in the tree tops and one round, luckily a dud, landed in a crowded ward. On April 22nd, finally, several shells hit in one of the wards and mess halls, killing or wounding about a score of prisoners, and Gillespie was forced to empty his more exposed wards to avoid further casualties. Again and again he protested to Sekiguchi—without success. The Japanese army was busy fighting the war, said Sekiguchi, and nobody would leave the hospital until after Corregidor had fallen.

The general treatment of the prisoners at Hospital No. 2, as elsewhere on Bataan, varied with the individual. Food and medicine were scarce, although the Japanese finally issued some rice. Looting continued and a few men were beaten. Fortunately, all the nurses had been able to get away to Corregidor on the night of April 8th, but one American woman, the only female patient in the hospital was brutally raped. When Colonel Gillespie reported this to Major Sekiguchi, the Japanese officer was surprisingly sympathetic for the first time and promised drastic action. But as far as the Americans could see, nothing was done.

With these exceptions, however, there were no cases of physical maltreatment. Many of the Japanese limited themselves to verbal abuse of the Americans and some wefe even quite friendly. Considerable barter took place between prisoners and guards. During these exchanges, the Japanese displayed an unexpected sense of fairness and honesty. Hardly a day went by, also, without visits by two or more curious Japanese officers engaged in sightseeing. Each one carried at least one camera and there was a great deal of snapping of pictures.

Many of the Americans were allowed to forage for themselves. Some of them discovered a large pile of American rations in the woods near the hospital, an additional source of food to be tapped without the knowledge of the Japanese. A few of the men out foraging even managed to take advantage of their freedom and escape to Corregidor.

On May 11th, a few days after the fall of the island, the 600 bed patients at Hospital No. 2 and many of the medical personnel were transferred to General Hospital No. 1. Five valuable truckloads of vital medical supplies also made the move—against the orders and without the knowledge of the good Major Sekiguchi. A few days later, the ambulatory cases and remaining staff members were transferred to a prison camp in central Luzon. As they drove north, the pajama-clad bodies of many of the Filipino patients who had left the hospital so precipitously five weeks earlier could still be seen alongside the road.

9

The Massacre of the 91st Division

On April 11th, once the surrender of the I Corps was completed, the Filipino and American troops in western Bataan began their slow assembly. From the front lines south of the Pilar-Bagac road and from the jungle slopes of the Mariveles Mountains, they straggled in disorganized groups to the West Road. Then they went either north or south, to Bagac or Mariveles, an uncoordinated mass of men and vehicles moving with little direction from the Japanese.

Above the town of Mariveles, the West Road was clogged with troops going south. "There was no order," reported an American officer who participated in this movement, "as they were just streaming back." Most of the men were on foot, but many were riding in trucks, either on orders from or with the tacit approval of their captors.

The Japanese were completely unpredictable. Sometimes there were none to be seen. At other times they made their presence felt by shouting orders, or beating or looting the prisoners. In yet other instances they distributed cigarettes to their captives and behaved so well that an American enlisted man could write in his diary that the Japanese were "really nice to us." There seemed to be no pattern to their behavior.

Brigadier General Luther Stevens, one of Jones' subordinate commanders, and another American officer were riding south in their staff car. Suddenly a Japanese officer halted the sedan, threw open the door, and kicked and beat the two passengers out onto the ground. As they staggered to their feet, a truckload of American officers stopped behind the staff car and the Japanese began to strike at these men with a long bamboo pole. Just as suddenly he stopped, ordered Stevens and his companion into the truck, and walked off and left them. The truck went on toward Mariveles, only to be stopped again by other Japanese, who pulled the Americans off, tied them together in pairs, untied them, and then tied them again. Stevens and the others spent the night tightly bound in the woods near the road. In the morning, the guards removed the ropes and a Japanese colonel explained that tying the men up had been "a mistake." After a small breakfast, the prisoners resumed the trip to Mariveles, this time on foot.

Those I Corps troops closer to Bagac than Mariveles moved north to Bagac, experiencing much the same sort of uneven and unpredictable treatment. One Filipino regiment was assembled in a large group. The Japanese directed the prisoners to place their arms in a single large pile, and then separated the Filipino enlisted men from their American officers. They next proceeded to search the Filipinos, relieve them of their watches and money, and then marched them away to Bagac. The Americans, about thirty in number, were not touched that day, but the next morning the Japanese stole most of their possessions and directed them to walk to Bagac. Here the officers were assembled in a dry rice field and left alone for the night. So far, except for the loss of their personal effects, they had not been mistreated. Colonel Virgil N. Cordero, the regimental commander, recalls that he said to himself, "Things are going to be all right after all. They are going to take good care of us."

He changed his mind the next day when he and his fellow officers were forced to strip to their undershorts and repair a demolished bridge on the West Road. A Japanese guard stood by, armed with a club. When he was in any way dissatisfied with the quality or speed of the work, he would indicate his displeasure with his club. The men quickly learned that it was better to do things his way.

Within a few days after the surrender, most of the troops in western Bataan had either reached or passed through Mariveles or Bagac on their way to Balanga. This was already somewhat behind the original Japanese schedule for moving the prisoners and demonstrated at once how unrealistic this plan was.

The troops traveling to Balanga along the Pilar-Bagac road generally made the march by themselves, unguarded by Japanese soldiers. Most of the Filipino members of the 11th Philippine Army Division were in this category. Assembled at Bagac, they were thoroughly searched and stripped of all personal possessions, blankets, and helmets, and then organized into groups of 100. The Japanese presented each group leader with a flag bearing Japanese characters, presumably as identification, and directed the men to walk to Balanga themselves. During their two days at Bagac the Filipinos had received nothing but biscuits and water, but the guards now gave each man some rice before he left.

The march along the Pilar-Bagac road was almost pleasant. The hot rays of the sun were deflected or filtered by the trees and heavy foliage that lined the way. The tension and horror of the battle for Bataan seemed far away, and the men began to relax a little for the first time in months. Without any Japanese guards to hurry them, they set their own pace, picking and eating sugar cane and wild vegetables and drinking from tiny streams.

Soon they crossed the Pantingan River, flowing north from the Mariveles Mountains, and crossed into the former II Corps sector. Now the pleasant sights of western Bataan were replaced by a more grisly view, for here the Good Friday offensive had wreaked its greatest carnage, and the devastated battlefield lay raw and ugly before their eyes. The men walked carefully around gaping shell holes, wrecked equipment, and putrifying corpses. As hungry as they had been before, they quickly lost their appetite. "Seeing so many bloated uniformed bodies—both Americans and Filipinos —had sickened us," recalled one Filipino officer.

Americans had similar experiences. The thirty officers with Colonel Cordero stayed at Bagac for two days, without food and sleeping on the ground. On April 14th, finally, they were given some rice and allowed to refill their canteens and then sent on their way along the Pilar-Bagac road. Like the

Filipinos of the 11th Division, they found that the absence of Japanese guards made the walk almost pleasant. They too sought the sweet and energizing sugar cane and the tasty wild vegetables of the forest. The Japanese had not given them any identifying flags, but Colonel Stuart MacDonald, the ranking American, carried a written pass to show to any Japanese troops they might encounter. This possibly saved them from physical punishment, but not from occasional annoyance. Although they had been stripped of almost all their possessions before they left Bagac, they were still searched by each Japanese soldier who inspected MacDonald's pass. It was a rare occasion when the searcher did not find something that struck his fancy.

At the Pantingan River the men stopped to rest. They tore the shoes from their hot, blistered feet and plunged into the water, clothes and all. For nearly half an hour they soaked themselves in the cool Pantingan. Then hunger reminded them to cook their rice and eat it. In the early afternoon, considerably refreshed, they again resumed their march and reached Balanga that evening. Without hurrying they had covered the fifteen miles from Bagac in one day and were none the worse for the hike.

If the walk along the Pilar-Bagac road was relatively pleasant, the trip across Bataan on another route proved to be horribly tragic. Most of the troops of the 91st Philippine Army Division were separated from their American officers and assembled on an east-west trail that ran generally parallel to the Pilar-Bagac road and several miles to its south. At about noon on April 11th, these men and a few stragglers from other units were directed to proceed along this trail to the East Road, a movement not in accordance with the original Japanese plan, but considerably shorter than the long trek through Mariveles. It would have been easier and quicker, however, for the men to have gone through Bagac. Taking that route might also have saved their lives.

Moving on foot and in trucks, without guards, the 91st Division troops advanced slowly. By nightfall they had reached the Pantingan River, where they were halted by a partially demolished bridge. The next morning they repaired the bridge and crossed the river, losing their trucks, however, to Japanese soldiers moving through the area.

By ten o'clock the Filipinos had covered two miles, when they were suddenly halted by other Japanese soldiers. These soldiers followed the usual practice of searching the prisoners and then separated the officers from the enlisted men.

At about noon, a Japanese officer, identified by one of the guards as Lieutenant General Akira Nara, 65th Brigade commander, arrived by automobile. The chances are that it was indeed Nara, for this was the very area occupied by his troops and the Japanese soldiers then present must have been from the 65th Brigade. A slender, bespectacled man, Nara held a quick conference with his officers and then drove off as quickly as he had come.

There is no record of what Nara said, but no sooner had he left than all Filipino officers and noncommissioned officers in the group, about 350 to 400 men, were lined up along the trail. The Filipino privates were ordered to continue east, but the rest of the captives were formed into three groups and their wrists tied securely with double-strand telephone wire. Each group consisted of four columns of men, and the wrists of each man were linked to the man behind him.

When this process was completed, the Japanese soldiers marched the prisoners to a nearby ravine where they lined them up in four long columns. By now the intent of the Japanese was clear. The helpless Filipinos knew that they had only a few moments to live. As the unfortunate men stood with their backs to their captors, a Japanese civilian interpreter began to address them in Tagalog. "My friends," he said, "don't take it so hard. You must be patient. Had you surrendered earlier you would not have met this tragedy. We are doing this because many of our soldiers died fighting against you. If you have any request before we kill you, ask it now."

As the interpreter finished his explanation, many of the men began to beg for their lives. But their pleas were ignored. One sergeant cried out that he should be spared because his mother was Japanese. The interpreter tried to intercede for him, but the Japanese commander refused to listen and the other officers began to draw their swords in anticipation of the coming slaughter. Seeing that there was no hope of saving many lives, Major Pedro L. Felix asked that the men be killed by machine gun or rifle fire and that they be allowed to face their executioners. This too was denied. While all this was going on, some of the Japanese soldiers who had gathered to watch gave the doomed men cigarettes. One Japanese even offered a crucifix to be kissed.

Then, at a given signal, the execution began. Japanese officers moved down the line from one end, mercilessly beheading the luckless Filipinos with their gleaming sabers. From the other end, the Japanese enlisted men worked toward them, methodically plunging their bayonets into the backs of the prisoners. Almost every thrust of sword or bayonet drew a scream of pain from its victim. For two hours the grisly slaughter continued, the Japanese sweating at their work in the hot sun, pausing to wipe away the perspiration, and then returning to their grim task. The agonized cries of the Filipinos were punctuated by the grunts of the Japanese as they thrust their bayonets home or swung their heavy swords through the air. If a single bayonet thrust or sword slash did not kill a man, he would be struck again and again until dead.

Suddenly, in the midst of the slaughter, the sergeant who had claimed that his mother was Japanese shouted at the top of his voice, "To hell with all of you Japanese! Come back here and kill us thoroughly!" A Japanese soldier ran over to him, thrust his bayonet repeatedly into the prostrate victim, and then, still not satisfied, fired three shots into his body.

When the massacre was over only half a dozen prisoners, all badly wounded in several places, remained alive. Buried beneath their slain comrades, they lay unnoticed by the Japanese, not daring to move.

One of these was Major Felix. Standing in the first row of captives, he had received four cruel bayonet wounds. The first thrust hit his shoulder blade and, as he screamed in pain, the second cut through his back and into his intestine. He dropped to his side and felt two more burning slashes as the bayonet thrust again and again into his body. Then the Japanese executioner, assuming his victim was dead, moved on to the next man.

Felix lay still, determined not to cry out and attract attention. As the man beside him threshed in agony, he threw his legs over Felix's head, then suddenly died. Felix was now concealed from the view of the executioners, and could breathe more openly and move his eyes. Never losing consciousness, he lay still, petrified by the thought that the Japanese might come back and finish him.

It was nightfall before the last of the Japanese soldiers had left the area and its company of bloody corpses. In the silent darkness, Felix slowly raised his head and looked around him. Unable to move because of his wounds and the telephone wire around his wrists, he was thirsty and in terrible agony. Almost out of his mind with pain, he decided to end it all and pressed his face into the ground, trying to smother himself. He soon gave this up, however, and began to consider his predicament. Carefully bracing himself with his feet, he placed his mouth to the wires connecting him with his comrades and, after several difficult hours, managed to gnaw through them. By this time, he discovered another officer who had somehow escaped death. Felix's hands were still tied behind his back, but he painfully dragged himself over to the other man. Working together, the two were able to free each other. Then they crawled, rolled, and clawed their agonized way across the ground—twenty or thirty feet at a time was all they could cover before they had to stop and rest—until finally the other officer died.

Felix went on alone. In the morning he met three others who had also escaped. One man had a huge sword slash across the back of his head, exposing his brain. He lived only a few days. Another had lost an ear and was severely cut in the neck and shoulder. The men bathed their wounds in a stream, ate fruit and leaves and tiny snails, and began to work their way toward the coast. Joined by another escapee, the wounded Filipinos wandered through central Bataan for nearly a week before they met some farmers who hid them and nursed them. Eventually Felix and the others were able to make their way out of Bataan and reach their homes near Manila.

The massacre of the Filipino officers and noncoms of the 91st Division was apparently the only mass execution to take place on Bataan. Indeed, there is no evidence that such a slaughter, organized and led by Japanese officers and methodically carried out, occurred anywhere else in the Philippines at this time.

Why it took place here is an unsolved riddle. One other incident may be related, however. Well before daylight on the morning of April 6th, at the height of the Good Friday offensive, counterattacking Filipino troops surprised and overran a 65th Brigade bivouac area, bayoneting those Japanese who lay asleep. The execution of the 91st Division troops—apparently by men from the 65th Brigade—took place barely three miles south of this bivouac area, and may well have been motivated by a desire for revenge. Ironically, it was a part of the 41st Division, rather than the 91st, that had been the attacking force on the 6th.

The role of General Nara—if indeed it was he—is difficult to understand. A graduate of the American Army's Infantry School at Fort Benning, Georgia, and a former student at Amherst College, he would seem the least likely type of Japanese to order such a massacre. Yet the probability cannot be ignored that it was General Nara who appeared just before the execution and that, if he did not actually order it to take place, presumably he must have known it was about to happen. Yet in the postwar trials of Japanese war criminals, Nara was not charged.

Whoever was responsible for the slaughter of the helpless Filipinos, it was without a doubt the worst single atrocity to take place on Bataan.

10

Up from Mariveles

The port town of Mariveles was the initial assembly point for most of the troops of the Luzon Force. On the morning of King's surrender the greater part of the Americans and Filipinos near the southern tip of Bataan were moving toward Mariveles. Some were probably acting on orders from their unit commanders, but most of them were headed south in hopes of getting a boat and escaping to Corregidor or because they had heard that they were to surrender near Mariveles.

By the afternoon of April 9th, when the first Japanese units reached the town, hordes of Filipino and American soldiers had already assembled there. Others were pouring in rapidly. All were apprehensive about their fate, but a Japanese general assured Brigadier General William E. Brougher that he need have no fears. "The Japanese fight very hard," he told Brougher, "but we hold no vindictiveness toward a defeated foe. We have our code we call *Bushido*. You will be well treated."

By six in the evening, enough Japanese were in Mariveles to begin rounding up the American and Filipino troops in the area. Some of the Japanese took food away from the prisoners, but initially there was no widespread looting. One group of captives, organized in a short time by the Japanese, began marching toward Balanga at once. The men walked slowly, unhurried by their guards, and took nearly five hours to cover the less than ten miles to Cabcaben, the first resting point. Stopping here shortly before midnight, the column was joined by other men taken prisoner in the immediate area. The Japanese issued no food to their captives, and the thirsty men were allowed only what water they could get from a nearby carabao wallow.

After about two hours, the march began again. As the column moved slowly north, one man suddenly broke ranks and ran to drink from a well. A Japanese guard dashed after him and swiftly bayoneted him to the ground. The rest of the prisoners kept on, halting to rest or sleep from time to time, and finally reached Balanga in midafternoon on April 11th. This was probably the first large body of prisoners to enter the town. Despite the slowness of the pace from Mariveles, the lack of food and the poor physical condition of the men proved too much for about a score of them. Barely able to stagger along the last few miles, they collapsed and died just as the group reached Balanga. The dead men were buried where they fell.

Other captives also left the Mariveles area on the night of the 9th, but most of the men did not begin to move out until the next day. Columns of prisoners continued to leave until the 17th, and it was April 23rd, two weeks after King's surrender, before the last of the men departed. As a result, arrivals at Balanga—and later at Camp O'Donnell—were similarly staggered.

In the confusion of Bataan's surrender, the American guns on Corregidor proved an unexpected hazard to the prisoners in southern Bataan. At about four o'clock on the afternoon of the 9th, Japanese artillerymen set up a battery of 75's on the beach near Cabcaben and began to shell Corregidor. The guns were in the open, clearly visible from the island, and American return fire quickly destroyed them. Unfortunately, however, it also killed or wounded nearly two dozen prisoners assembled nearby.

On Corregidor, meanwhile, General Wainwright was unaware of this tragedy. But he realized the danger to American and Filipino troops still in southern Bataan and quickly ordered the artillery out of action. Despite increasingly heavy shelling by Japanese guns on Bataan, he maintained this restriction until the 12th. Then, believing that all the captured men except those in the two general hospitals had been evacuated from the danger zone, he authorized counterbattery fire against enemy targets that could be definitely located. Wainwright directed his artillery commanders to take extreme care not to hit the hospitals and furnished them with maps of Bataan on which the hospital areas had been clearly marked. Corregidor's guns fired hundreds of rounds at targets around these areas, but only occasionally did shells come close enough to inflict casualties on the hospitalized prisoners.

After the war, General Wainwright wrote that he did not authorize artillery fire against Bataan until the 15th. Yet Corregidor's artillery records and the testimony of American prisoners on Bataan show clearly that he lifted his restriction on the 12th.

This action came too soon. On the same day, Filipino and American troops marching past another Japanese artillery position at Cabcaben came under fire from Corregidor's guns. Fortunately no one was hurt, and the guards quickly hustled the prisoners out of the danger zone. But on the 13th, artillery fire from Corregidor killed some Americans. More were wounded in the days that followed. Private First Class George A. Cecil and about one hundred others were in the impact area of the American shells. Ignoring the Japanese guards, Cecil said later, "We just got up and left." But several men in the group were hit.

The exodus of the prisoners from southern Bataan was a disorganized and confused one. Many were marched back and forth in aimless fashion until they became thoroughly mystified over which way they were actually heading. One group of men, rounded up above Cabcaben on the morning of the 10th, was left sitting in the hot sun beside the East Road without food or water until midafternoon. Then the prisoners were formed into a column of twos and marched, not north toward Balanga, but south. This group walked no more than a few hundred yards when it met a similar column from Mariveles, hiking in the opposite direction. For a moment the road was completely blocked. Then, after some confusion, the two columns of prisoners became a single one, and moved off again to the north.

The day was hot and dry and the road dusty and clogged with traffic. In the ditches on both sides was strewn the litter of war: burned trucks, battered artillery pieces, rifles, abandoned equipment, and an occasional rotting body. On the road itself the prisoners faced a never-ending stream of traffic as Japanese troops pushed south on foot, astride horses, or in trucks, accompanied by heavy cumbersome artillery pieces. Hundreds of Filipino civilian refugees seeking desperately to find their way north added to the jam and confusion.

The prisoners wound their way as best they could through this traffic. Sometimes the column of tired men would be on the road, passing between files of Japanese infantry or dodging trucks. The Japanese soldiers riding in those trucks were an added hazard, for they occasionally swung at the captives with bamboo poles. At other times, the line of prisoners walked beside the road, jumping ditches, climbing up and down higher ground, and avoiding abandoned equipment. The marchers would move forward for a while, then be stopped for traffic, then move again, then come to a halt. This slow, irregular process continued for several hours, tiring further the already weak and exhausted men. Some time after darkness the whole column was turned about and countermarched to Cabcaben, where the prisoners spent the night before starting all over again in the morning.

The Japanese guards, it seemed clear, were often confused about just what to do with their captives. Some even informed the prisoners, apparently in good faith, that the captured men were going to Manila, where the Filipinos would be released to rejoin their families. They would be free, explained a Japanese captain to a Filipino colonel, because "we are all brother officers, and of the same color."

Actually, nothing of the sort took place. Instead the prisoners became more and more confused by their guards' inconsistencies. When one group reached Cabcaben, the men were led off the road, apparently to camp for the night. Hardly had they broken ranks when their guards suddenly became excited and rushed in among them, driving the bewildered prisoners back into line with shouts and blows with their rifle butts. The captives were then marched on for another four miles to Lamao, where they finally halted for the night.

Still another column reached Cabcaben at nightfall. The men had marched all day under brutal Japanese guards who allowed them a single two-hour rest period in the hot sun, and who gave them neither food nor water. Halted in a muddy rice paddy just above the town, the exhausted prisoners had just flung themselves down in the mire to sleep when they were awakened and kicked to their feet by the guards. Back south they marched for an hour or so and then once again turned north until, in the small hours of the morning, they finally stopped just a short distance from the rice field where they had first halted.

There seemed no reason for this night march. Now the Japanese guards, who must have been getting fairly tired themselves, allowed their worn-out charges to rest and to fill their canteens from a brackish carabao wallow. Then they crowded the men into a small field so jammed with prisoners that no one could stretch himself out and lie down. Everyone had to sit, leaning on his neighbor, and get what sleep he could in that position. At dawn the stiff, tired men were ordered to their feet and once more headed north.

Now there was no longer any appearance of an orderly formation. The men slogged forward, head bowed, putting one foot before the other. Hunger and exhaustion had so numbed them that they moved like automatons, without will or reason. Some of the prisoners, delirious with fever or burning thirst, suffered hallucinations and were tantalized by mirages. More and more of them began to drop by the wayside, and as they did fear and despair began to grip the others. Each man began to wonder how long it would be before he, too, would stumble and fall and rise no more.

Halts for rest came at odd intervals. But they were always welcome. Each moment the weary captives could relax their tortured bodies and aching legs seemed a precious bit of heaven amidst an incredible hell. Often, however, starting up again after a halt was more painful than the march itself had ever been. One group of prisoners was lucky enough to have a five- or ten-minute break regularly every hour and a half when the guards were changed. Others were given a respite only during the hottest part of the day, and some of these men had to march all night. And many prisoners who were permitted to sleep through the night were then forced to walk steadily all day without any break at all.

The treatment of the prisoners usually varied with the Japanese guards, some of whom were "less inconsiderate," as one American sergeant put it, than others. On the morning of April 10th, quite a few Americans were assembled on a small hill just off the East Road. Several times during the day the Japanese guards took them down the hill for water, then finally decided that the men were not going to escape, and allowed them to go back and forth themselves. Farther up the road, Colonel Ernest B. Miller was leading a column of weary prisoners. When he explained to the guards that the men behind him were worn out and sick, the Japanese proved to be courteous and understanding. They allowed frequent rests and even permitted the captives to forage for food. Another column of prisoners was pleasantly surprised when a Japanese soldier, riding past the men in a truck, tossed them several bottles of soft drinks and a few packs of cigarettes. "The Japanese were kind and helpful to us," wrote one Filipino in his diary.

Yet there were incidents in sharp contrast to these: beatings, lootings, killings.

Lieutenant Joseph F. Boyland was held at Mariveles for three days and questioned about Corregidor. When he refused to answer, his captors beat him, tortured him with a knife, and refused him food and water. Finally he was released and pushed into the line of march. Master Sergeant Michael H. Bruaw saw a group of Japanese soldiers using several Filipinos for bayonet practice, plunging their sharp weapons repeatedly into their screaming victims. Further along, a column of prisoners was plodding up the road when a Japanese army truck appeared on the scene. Suddenly—and deliberately, it seemed to the captives—the driver drove the truck directly into the marching men. Most of them jumped clear, but several were run down and killed or badly hurt. The injured somehow managed to regain their feet and stumbled forward with their companions. The dead remained where they fell.

In the general confusion, some prisoners hiked all the way to Balanga without any guards, others were guarded only a part of the way. On those fortunate occasions when there were no Japanese to accompany them, the prisoners could set their own rate of march and stop to rest or forage whenever they wished. But often the unguarded groups were halted by passing Japanese troops who beat the men without provocation and looted them of everything save the clothes on their backs.

What was left of an artillery battalion of American and Philippine Scouts began driving up the East Road in several American trucks. They had gone only a few miles when Japanese troops stopped them and ordered them to continue on foot. As the men walked along, other Japanese soldiers constantly halted them to search for souvenirs and other items. Finally, they reached an open field where large numbers of Filipinos and Americans were being assembled, searched, and looted. Here they stayed for nearly twenty-four hours. The Japanese issued no food or water to their captives, but the Scouts were able to leave the field and forage for provisions for themselves and the Americans. They brought back water as well as some canned food they had found in a nearby abandoned supply area. Many took advantage of this opportunity to escape. Changing into civilian clothes, which for some reason they still carried in their packs, they melted into the jungle or simply walked north along the road, usually unmolested by the Japanese who assumed that they were civilians.

There were no latrine facilities and the American officers had great difficulty in explaining to their Japanese guards that they wanted to leave the field to relieve themselves. Finally, after some rather explicit sign language, they made themselves understood. "Ah," said one Japanese officer, "W. C.!" Things were somewhat easier after this.

The next day the trek continued. At rest periods the guards sometimes allowed the men to get water; sometimes they refused. At no time did they give them any food. Fortunately, the pace of the march was slow.

But many prisoners who made the journey to Balanga under constant guard soon learned that their captors were usually anxious to move them north as fast as possible. In one column the guards were changed every three miles or so, and each new set of guards forced the prisoners to double-time for more than a mile after the change. Other groups were forced to double-time at uncoordinated intervals, seemingly at the whim of the individual Japanese accompanying them. Sometimes the guards rode bicycles and the prisoners were forced to dog trot just to keep up with them. In still other groups a period of double-timing would be followed by a longer one in which the men were forced to creep along at a snail's pace so slow that it seemed more tiring than running.

Colonel John Ball was leading one column of prisoners. The tired and hungry men behind him, many of them suffering from malaria or dysentery, had eaten nothing since the previous morning. For this group, then, even a slow pace was difficult to maintain. But if the colonel tried to lessen his speed, the nearest Japanese guard ordered him to hurry. The men behind Ball would then cry out for him to slow down, and he would ease his pace. Again the guard would tell him to walk faster, Ball would obey, the men in the column would complain, and he would decrease his speed. "This happened several times," recalled Ball, "and the last time the Japanese hollered at me again and came over and hit me with the butt of the rifle over the head, and I went down."

At times the Japanese guards seemed almost frenzied in their attempts to keep up the pace of the marching columns. Time after time prisoners who straggled or fell out of line would be shot, bayoneted, or beaten to death. Their comrades watched horrified, helpless to do anything, and wondering if they themselves might be next.

Some exhausted stragglers were even buried alive, often by other prisoners who were forced at bayonet point to carry out this grisly task. One dying Filipino, rolled into an open ditch for burial, was revived by the water standing at the bottom and tried to stand up. A Japanese soldier kicked him back into his grave and motioned for the horrified American who was burying him to hurry up.

When rest periods were allowed the marching men, there were always a few prisoners who were slow in getting to their feet. Then the guards rushed in and hurried them along with kicks or blows with their rifle butts. To Captain George W. Kane, it seemed as if the Japanese got "some animal pleasure" out of beating the men.

Sometimes the guards summarily bayoneted or shot any laggards. Even men who stopped to relieve themselves were shot without warning. One American was seized with an attack of acute appendicitis. A medical officer asked permission to stop and help him, but his request was refused and the stricken man was left to his fate. The doctor himself was threatened for his efforts.

One column of prisoners was followed by a truck carrying

Japanese soldiers. When one of the marching men fell to the ground, the guards ignored him, but the Japanese on the truck reached down and clubbed the helpless prisoner with their rifles. Sometimes they would leap down and bayonet the prostrate form. Prisoners in another column who dropped out of line were dispatched by a squad of Japanese riflemen marching just behind them, apparently for that specific purpose.

Whether the captives were allowed to assist their weaker comrades depended entirely on the whim of the guards. Some allowed it; others did not. In one long column of Filipinos, the stronger men carried their sick or wounded compatriots in improvised litters. But elsewhere an attempt to aid an exhausted comrade who could not keep up might bring death for both helper and friend.

Before long some of the Americans devised a system for aiding straggling companions without actually appearing to do so. For the most part, they tried to urge the weary men on with sharp words of encouragement, or perhaps by a joke or some light banter. Occasionally, they could offer a guiding hand or reach out and give the straggler a quick push forward.

Still, the sickest and most exhausted prisoners continued to fall. They dropped individually or by twos and threes, struggled to rise, or crawled forward on knees and elbows, punctuating their efforts with groans and hoarse breathing. Some managed to get up. Others remained where they had fallen, their faces pressed to the ground, dying or already dead. Most of the men who made the march from Bataan will never forget this sight.

11

The End of Phase I

Along the line of march from Mariveles to Balanga, the ranks of the prisoners were constantly swelled as other Luzon Force troops, captured inland, came down the many Bataan trails to the coastal road. Crowds of Filipino civilians also fell in line and mixed with the soldiers, increasing even more the size of the jagged columns that stumbled along the East Road in growing disorder. Groups that had left Mariveles numbering 300 now sometimes contained twice as many men. And as the prisoners moved farther north, they became more and more disorganized and increasingly difficult to control. The Japanese guards, faced with a growing number of captives to watch, grew nervous and lost their tempers more readily as they hurried their charges along.

The Japanese first attempted to impose some organization on the prisoners at Limay and, farther north, Orion. At these towns, they separated the thoroughly disorganized captives into groups of Americans, Filipino troops, and Filipino civilians. Then the prisoners were further divided into units of 100 and lined up in a column of fours. The Japanese picked one man, usually an officer, to lead each group. Then they ordered the captives to begin marching north.

As usual, there was little consistency in the movement. Japanese guards walked or rode bicycles alongside some of the captives. Other prisoners marched alone. And, although the 14th Army plan had not foreseen that any transportation would be available below Balanga, some of the men were able to ride.

At Limay, the Japanese announced to one group that all prisoners who were captains or higher would ride in trucks. Colonel Albert R. Ives, the senior artilleryman in the group, directed all high-ranking artillery officers to share their insignia with those men who would otherwise have to walk. Well over 200 officers and some of the more fortunate enlisted men boarded trucks and rode in relative comfort to Balanga.

Many Filipino soldiers and civilians had driven all the way from Mariveles in trucks and buses. Now Japanese troops stopped some of these trucks, forced the prisoners down, threw their baggage in the ditch, and ordered them to continue on foot. A truckload of Americans was stopped on the road at Orion. A Japanese interpreter told the men to jump out one by one. As each prisoner landed on the ground, Japanese soldiers shouting *"bakayaro"* ("stupid idiot") clubbed him with heavy wooden sticks.

The Japanese troops used the staging points at Limay and Orion to good advantage. Whenever a group of prisoners came to a halt, there was ample opportunity for their captors to steal whatever personal possessions were still left to the helpless men. Even before they reached Limay, the prisoners were subject to countless searches. They quickly learned that the Japanese is as avid a collector of souvenirs as any other soldier in the world. And on Bataan the Japanese troops were after booty as well. "At breakfast I saw my first Jap," wrote one American in his diary shortly after the surrender. "He was looting."

In the five days it took this man to reach Balanga, he was searched at least seven times. Another prisoner, who took a little longer to get there, found himself the subject of Japanese searches no less than a dozen times. And for still others, the search was almost a continuous process. Some were systematically searched every time the Japanese changed guards, others were gone over by every Japanese they met on the road.

Frequently the guards made no attempt to steal from their charges, but passing Japanese soldiers often helped themselves freely whenever the prisoners halted for any length of time. At one point, Japanese noncoms had spread blankets on the ground and were ordering all Americans and Filipinos who walked by to drop their money and jewelry on the blankets. Several Japanese privates stood a few yards up the road. They searched each prisoner as he came to them, and it went hard with him if he held anything back from the blanket.

Private Zoeth Skinner's group was carrying its own luggage when it stopped for the night. In the morning, the men left their bags on the ground while they lined up to be counted. The guards then told them to go back and get their equipment but, even in this short interval, Skinner's bag had already been "well looted," as he put it later, "and nothing was left."

For the Japanese soldiers, used to a frugal military life, many of the everyday articles carried by the prisoners must have seemed like luxuries indeed. "My old toothbrush, already unserviceable," recalled one Filipino, "was avidly taken away from me by a big-bellied Japanese cook." Master Sergeant James Baldasarre lost his shoes to a looter, but took another pair from the feet of a dead Filipino. One Japanese soldier seized an American colonel's eyeglasses. He tried them on, said "Ah," and walked away wearing them.

The Japanese were most interested in such prizes as pens, watches, knives, rings, cigarettes, razors, and money. Also on the list of desirable booty were choice items like hats, shirts, blankets, spare uniforms, insignia of rank, soap, and even playing cards and personal photographs and letters. Staff Sergeant Donald N. Smith found himself being stripped of his dogtags. Another American sergeant was severely beaten when a Japanese discovered two .45-caliber cartridges in his pocket. And anyone who tried to conceal a pistol was lucky to escape with just a beating.

The main object of all these searches was loot. Many of the Japanese were ostensibly looking for weapons, but they were primarily after booty. Curiously enough, the Japanese never checked the prisoners for documents that might have been of intelligence value, and rarely even interrogated them. Diaries, orders, plans, manuals, maps and photographs, pay books, or any other records could well have provided a great variety of useful information. But the Japanese made no attempt to find material of this sort. Indeed, only with Gen-

BATAAN
THE MARCH OF DEATH
A SHATTERING SAGA OF
HORROR AND HEROISM

Starting the Death March.

Lt. Gen. Masaharu Homma.

During the March these prisoners were photographed. They have their hands tied behind their backs.

A group of American prisoners resting while a Japanese soldier stands guard.

Some exhausted prisoners are allowed a brief rest during the March.

Under Japanese guard the American POW's sort U.S. equipment. Following this the Death March began.

An American officer being interrogated by his captors.

General King surrenders to Col. Motoo Nakayama. From left to right: Col. Everett C. Williams, Maj. Gen. Edward P. King, Jr., Maj. Wade Cothran, and Capt. Achile C. Tisdale.

eral King and a limited number of others did 14th Army staff officers make any attempt at interrogation. And then the main purpose of their questions was to elicit details of the fortifications and dispositions on Corregidor. A few questions were motivated by curiosity about the fighting on Bataan. But there was no systematic attempt to gather intelligence, either on Bataan or later in prison camp. When Japanese soldiers went through the pockets of their captives, they were strictly interested in plunder.

Nor was it wise to resist Japanese looters. The troops of one American unit had given their money to their commanding officer to hold for them. A Japanese soldier going through this officer's pockets had already taken his ring and watch when he discovered the money and pulled it out triumphantly. Protesting, the American tried to explain that the money belonged to his men. But his arguments were short. The Japanese soldier yanked him out of the line of prisoners, raised his rifle, and, before any of the other captives realized what was happening, shot him dead.

Another officer refused to surrender his ring. The Japanese guard searching him drew a bolo, slashed off the officer's finger, and removed the ring from the bloody digit. The shocked and bleeding American was pushed back into the line of march, dazed and stumbling.

Other prisoners did not make the same mistake after this object lesson. "We offered no objection to the Japanese," recalled a philosophical Filipino officer. "Who would anyway? It was their day and they should be quick to grasp its opportunities."

Yet, in the curious atmosphere that pervaded the area,

some Japanese could be argued out of taking loot. A few were even persuaded to return stolen goods. And others did not even steal in the first place. "I well recall the soldier," wrote Colonel Ray M. O'Day, "who looked at me and said, 'So sorry. So sorry!' It helped salve the shock of the losses."

Perhaps most tragic was the fate of those prisoners unfortunate enough to be caught by their captors with Japanese money or equipment in their possession. Regardless of how the prisoners had obtained these items, the Japanese invariably assumed that they had been taken from the bodies of 14th Army troops killed in battle. Sometimes this was true, but many of the prisoners had carried Japanese money as a souvenir even before the war, since it was readily available in the Philippines. Others were unlucky enough to own shaving mirrors or other items that bore the inscription MADE IN JAPAN. One American captain had a small fan given him by a sympathetic guard, and this too aroused his captors.

Many of these men were severely beaten. Major Fred R. Castro, a Filipino who spoke Japanese, was pressed into service as an interpreter by Japanese troops searching a group of prisoners. One of the searchers discovered some Japanese shoestrings in the possession of an American soldier. Through Castro, he asked where the soldier had obtained them. The American had taken them from the feet of a dead Japanese, but he and Castro invented a story that the shoestrings had been secured in an exchange with a Japanese guard. Unfortunately, the Japanese who had discovered the shoestrings did not believe the story. He raised his bayoneted rifle and would have run the American through if Castro had not succeeded in talking him out of it. Instead, the Japanese guards ordered the soldier to take off his clothes. Then they beat him mercilessly before sending him, stark naked, stumbling back to his companions.

The Japanese executed several Americans who were caught with Japanese goods. Some were shot, some beheaded, some beaten to death. A few of these were coin and currency collectors who died for their hobby.

At Mariveles, the guards discovered that an American captain had some Japanese yen notes. A big Japanese officer instantly threw the American to his knees, pulled his sword from his scabbard, and raised it with both hands high above his head. It glistened there for a moment, brightly in the sun, and then, while the other prisoners watched incredulously, the Japanese brought it down swiftly. It struck the captain on the back of the neck with a heavy thud, like a butcher's cleaver chopping into a large piece of meat. As the sword went through the neck and struck the ground, the head seemed to leap forward as if it had a life of its own. It hit the earth, bounced and, to the horror of the watching prisoners, rolled forward crazily amongst them. Meanwhile the captain's body had tumbled forward, the arms jerking, and the hands opening and closing jerkily. Blood spurted in great gushes from the gaping wound above the shoulders, turning the dusty white earth into dark red mud. Many of the other Americans could stand the sight no longer, and turned away. The whole incident had taken barely a few minutes.

Such Japanese cruelty was not the only torture with which the weary prisoners had to contend. The unbearable tropical heat increased their misery a thousandfold. April was the last month of the Philippine dry season, and the scorching rays of a brilliant sun beat down without mercy on the battle-scarred peninsula. Nearly half a year of dry heat had turned the earth to dust and withered the vegetation that covered the once green slopes of the mountains. Four months of air and artillery bombardment had further stripped Bataan of trees and foliage, and scarred and blackened stumps were all that remained in some once heavily forested areas. Here and there the woods were still ablaze from the last great Japanese bombardment. From these huge pyres, great clouds of smoke and heat arose, torturing the lungs of all who passed nearby. There was no breeze to stir the air or bring relief from the incessant heat and choking dust.

Beneath the burning sun, the prisoners stumbled along. Their weary steps raised a fog of chalk-like powder that hung in the heavy atmosphere, clung to their bodies, made their eyes smart and their lungs gasp, and turned their per-spiration-soaked beards almost white. Japanese infantry, trucks, and horse- and tractor-drawn artillery moved south along the same road, churning the dry earth and swirling dust until the prisoners were nearly blinded.

Marching in the heat and the dust was brutally exhausting, and the burning sun took its toll of the weaker men. Those who were fortunate enough to be wearing some sort of head covering stood the best chance of surviving its punishment. The lucky ones had fatigue hats or had fashioned turbans for themselves with towels or handkerchiefs. Many had thrown away their heavy helmets or had been ordered to turn them in at Mariveles. At one point along the road, a Japanese soldier armed with a long stick amused himself by knocking the helmets from the heads of any prisoners fortunate enough to be wearing them. The helpless men did not dare protest, and could only watch bitterly as their helmets rolled in the dust. Then they marched on under the burning sun.

One column of exhausted prisoners arrived at Limay during the day and was forced to sit in the open without protection. A Japanese officer informed them that they were being given the "sun treatment" as punishment for not having surrendered sooner. This same group received the "sun treatment" daily for the next week as it marched north, usually from two to four in the afternoon. Each "treatment" was preceded by a speech almost as sickening to some as the terrible heat. Many men passed out under the sun's unbearably hot rays, but there was no lessening of this torture. Those who collapsed were left on the ground when the column of prisoners resumed its march.

The officer who administered this treatment must have been operating on his own, since this was not a regular custom during the evacuation from Bataan. Many times groups of prisoners were forced to halt and wait in the sun, but in these instances the men were not ordered to remove their hats, nor were they told they were being punished, as was the case here. In one other instance, in northern Bataan, a Japanese officer administered the "sun treatment" to another group, to teach them "discipline," he said. But this appears to have been the only other case of such deliberate torture.

There was another, nauseating side effect of the heat. As the prisoners pushed on through the inferno of the day, the horrible odors and sights of the dead war impressed themselves on their sickened nostrils and burning eyes. Sun-blackened and bloated corpses lay scattered across the scarred battlefield, filling the air with a terrible stench. On some of the swollen human carcasses the horrified men could see big black crows fighting each other for chunks of meat that they tore off. Green flies, a million of them it seemed, hovered over the putrifying bodies. Sometimes prisoners in a column halted for the night would suddenly become aware of the smell of a rotting corpse and would hastily drag their exhausted bodies to another spot.

To the carrion odor of the dead was added the burnt smell of villages gutted by shellfire and bombs. The men plodded along the sunbaked road, trying not to breathe the sickening pungence that surrounded them, now and then stepping over bodies or mangled limbs, avoiding the sight of dying or dead prisoners in the ditch, and wondered if they were not indeed in another world. With heads bowed beneath the burning sun, mouth parched, eyes smarting, one leg mechanically moving ahead of another, they staggered on.

In the enervating heat and choking dust, water became an obsession. The men craved it so badly and thought about it so constantly that it even entered their dreams. How much water they were able to get depended on their guards, and here, as in most things, the attitude seemed to vary with the individual Japanese.

Along Bataan's East Road, and for some distance into central Luzon, were numerous artesian wells, many of them free-flowing. Their location was frequently indicated by a faucet atop a pipe rising a few feet from the ground, normally fairly convenient to the road. The Japanese allowed some of the prisoners to drink as much as they wanted at these wells, but usually forbade them from taking the time to fill their canteens. One guard firmly refused to let his captives hold their canteens beneath the faucet, then, a few minutes later, just as arbitrarily told them to go ahead. Other prisoners lost their canteens to looting Japanese. Or sometimes Japanese soldiers grabbed canteens and gave the water to their horses. Occasionally they just emptied them on the ground.

Some of the prisoners swear that they were given no water for days. Others were able to drink very little, sometimes only what they could get without the knowledge of the guards. One group of prisoners was denied water during its first day of captivity and was issued only a third of a canteenful on each day thereafter. Another group was allowed water on only three occasions during the entire trip to Camp O'Donnell. One fortunate American, Corporal L. Arhutick, managed to satisfy his thirst with six small cans of milk that he had found in Mariveles and which he had somehow kept hidden from the Japanese.

Thirst grew rapidly. So desperate were the men that they did not hesitate to drink the bacteria-filled water of stagnant pools, polluted streams, and muddy rice paddies or carabao wallows. They held their noses to seal off the sickening odor, but they drank all the water they could. Some were so thirsty that even the sight of swollen bodies floating in the water could not keep them from drinking. More than one man drank his fill, and then vomited in disgust at the sight and the smell. A few were fortunate to have held onto a bottle of iodine or some other disinfectant with which to purify the water. But most were not so lucky and suffered the consequences.

The sight of a well or pool of water along the route of march was often the signal for a wild dash to its side by the dehydrated men. Then the Japanese guards would run after the prisoners, kicking and hitting them or beating the helpless men with their rifle butts, until the captives were back in line again. Often the guards would charge with fixed bayonets, or simply fire their rifles at the thirsty prisoners. A few more bodies would be left beside the road.

At Lamao, groups of as many as 600 captives waded into the warm waters of Manila Bay and refreshed their debilitated bodies. Nobody seems to know whether the Japanese ever actually granted permission for this luxury. Usually they allowed it. But some prisoners were shot at as they stood refreshing themselves.

One night a brief but heavy tropical storm hit Bataan. At first, the captives welcomed the cooling water, but soon they were chilled to the bone and shivering violently in the downpour. Even then, their dehydrated bodies soaked up the rain so fast that in a few hours they were badly in need of water again.

As much as the prisoners suffered from lack of water, their need for food was almost as serious. The Japanese had made no provision for feeding their captives before the assembly at Balanga, but this was because the 14th Army plan had allowed only a day or less to complete this assembly. Since the trip to Balanga took longer for most of the men, they frequently went without food.

Nevertheless, many of the prisoners were fed something by their captors. Almost always it was rice, the basic item of the Japanese ration. The amount doled out varied from as little as a handful to as much as a bowl, sometimes even with a strip of bacon. A few prisoners were lucky enough to be given a can of captured American rations. In most cases, only a single issue of food was given each man, and sometimes there was not even enough for all the men in the group being fed. Some got nothing.

If the prisoners had their own food, the Japanese often allowed them to cook and eat it. Some of the captives walked along gnawing on raw turnips that they had been able to dig up during a rest halt. This was not "a substantial food," wrote one Filipino officer, but it "did the miracle of giving us a little strength to reach Balanga." Other men sometimes discovered stalks of sugar cane growing beside the road. The cane was a welcome treat, and a ready source of quick energy to the lucky finders.

As in other matters, treatment was apt to vary with the individual Japanese. The worst of these were the Japanese soldiers who saw fit to steal food from the captives. Many of the prisoners had been allowed to leave Mariveles carrying whatever food they happened to have with them, only to lose much of this to looting Japanese troops encountered on the road. Some prisoners were actually issued food at Mariveles but had to give it up when the guards were changed a little later.

Equally frustrating for the starving men was to march by a pile of captured American canned goods or to see any type of food being eaten by the Japanese. One group of Americans sat on one side of the East Road for several hours, watching some Japanese on the other side eating American

"C" rations—meat, vegetables, and crackers. Farther along, a column of prisoners was halted near a pile of captured canned goods. An elderly American colonel who had marched all day at the head of the group approached a guard. In sign language, he pleaded for the food to be given to the prisoners. The Japanese picked up the can in apparent acquiescence, then suddenly and brutally smashed it across the American's face, ripping open his cheek. The colonel stood there for a moment, blood running down his face and neck, then turned back to his men. He held his hands out, palms upward, in a helpless gesture of despair.

* * *

For many days after General King's surrender on April 9th, the prisoners poured into Balanga on foot and by truck. The length of time it took to reach the assembly point varied with each group of men. Some covered the distance in two days. Others were on the road for nearly a week. Large numbers of captives reached Balanga and pushed on to the north before many of their comrades even left Mariveles. By late April, most of the prisoners seem to have been evacuated from southern Bataan.

The first phase of the Japanese plan, the assembly at Balanga, proved in execution to be a dismal failure. It was disorganized, uncoordinated, inadequately supervised, frequently brutal, and marked by a cruel lack of discipline. Obviously, the original evacuation plan was inadequate, yet no significant adjustments were made when this became evident. The Japanese provided some food and transportation for their captives, but not enough. They failed completely to appreciate the incredibly poor physical condition of the prisoners and the difficulty of their transition from American command to prisoner of war status.

For the men who underwent this transition, it was a shocking, bewildering, and often fatal nightmare. The harassed captives saw and experienced events that tried their senses and overwhelmed their imaginations. Yet their arrival at Balanga was not the end of their trials. It only concluded the first phase of the tragic exodus from Bataan. From here to Camp O'Donnell, many of the prisoners would face their most severe trial.

IV
Horror Trek

12

Balanga

Once the captured men of the Luzon Force were assembled at Balanga, the Japanese planned to move them in easy stages to their final destination at Camp O'Donnell. This movement, Phase II of the plan, was supposed to be an orderly, well-regulated one in which, according to the 14th Army staff estimate, transportation would be available for about one-fourth of the prisoners. The remainder of the men would have to walk, but resting and feeding places would be set up along the route.

Yet, like Phase I, this part of the Japanese plan also broke down. The cumulative result was a tragedy so horrible that it has justly become known as the "Death March."

The town of Balanga was the capital of Bataan Province, with a prewar population of nearly 5,000. Most of the houses had been severely damaged by shellfire, and not a few were leveled almost to the ground. Here and there Filipino civilians, a small fraction of the inhabitants, had now begun to return. From the scattered wreckage and debris, they were attempting to restore their homes or, where this was impossible, to improvise some other shelter.

It was here that the prisoners were assembled in significant numbers for the first time. Japanese guards searched many of the captives as they arrived and relieved them of anything of value they might have retained. Then the men were assigned to assembly areas on all sides of the town. Usually, but not always, Filipinos and Americans were placed in separate groups. All around them they could see their fellow prisoners, a great mass of tired and ragged humanity that filled the entire area. As each man looked at the thin, wretched, dirty, unshaven creatures around him, he knew that he was seeing himself, and his spirits sank.

The makeshift quality and great variety of assembly areas at Balanga clearly showed the extent of Japanese unpreparedness to handle the tens of thousands of prisoners that poured into the town. These assembly points ranged in size from tiny yards to huge areas twelve acres large. Some of the captives were simply herded together in big, open, unfenced fields. Others were kept in smaller barbed-wire enclosures. One large group was put in the courtyard of an old building dating from the Spanish days which had somehow escaped destruction. Brigadier General Luther Stevens ended up in a cell in the town jail. Still other prisoners were so crowded that there was no room to stretch their legs. They sat doubled up, knees against their chins, hands clasped across their ankles, pressed as nearly as possible into the shape of a ball.

Throughout the area, groups of prisoners were constantly entering and leaving their enclosures. New columns of men arriving at Balanga milled about uncertainly as Japanese guards harangued them, shouted orders that no one understood, changed or contradicted these orders, beat and kicked the prisoners, and only added to the general confusion. None of the captives had any idea of who was in charge of things or of exactly what anyone was supposed to do.

In the crowded assembly areas, the effects of disease, especially dysentery, were horrible to see. Few, if any, provisions appear to have been made for the sanitary disposal of human refuse. Sick men who could not control their bowels defecated at will in the area. Ironically enough, those men not suffering from dysentery or diarrhea had had so little to eat that the problem of bowel control never arose for them. Some went as long as two weeks after the surrender without a bowel movement.

The Japanese allowed some of the prisoners to relieve themselves in a bamboo thicket. This area, one of the few shady places in the entire camp, was full of dead and dying men. The odor was repulsive, overwhelming. Colonel John H. Ball recalls that "the stench of the dead in that thicket prevented you from going in there unless you were just about to pass out, unless you were so sick that you didn't care anymore."

For the others, there was no such thing as leaving an enclosure to relieve themselves. Latrines, when they existed, were simply ditches running through or on the edge of the field. Where there were no ditches, the whole area was an open latrine.

As thousands upon thousands of men passed through Balanga, it became in short order a quagmire of filth and corruption. The smell and stain of diseased human waste covered the area like a fetid mist and hastened the spread of dysentery germs. Ordinarily flies and contaminated food and water will transmit dysentery, but now transmission directly from man to man was not uncommon. Those who died lay where they fell amidst the horrible filth and stench. In the heat, their bodies soon began to putrify and turn into fertile breeding places for maggots.

No medical facilities were offered by the Japanese. American doctors set up makeshift aid stations, but neither they nor their fellow prisoners had enough medicine to make any difference. Even if a man was relatively healthy when he reached Balanga, there was little chance that he would be altogether free from disease when he left.

Of the many who died at Balanga, not all succumbed entirely to disease. A number of Filipinos, too weak from sickness or hunger even to stand up, were given short shrift by their captors. Unwilling American and Filipino prisoners, Japanese bayonets at their backs, were forced to bury their ailing comrades alive. Sometimes a victim was already dead, but on other occasions the "dead man" would regain consciousness and attempt to climb out of his grave even as the dirt was being thrown on top of him. When this occurred, a Japanese guard would kick the dying prisoner back into the ground or force the horrified gravedigger to strike the victim with his shovel.

One dying Filipino, thrown prematurely into his grave, was aroused when the first shovelful of dirt struck his face.

He staggered to his feet, one hand raised before him, and said, "I am going to live. I am only weak. All I need is water." But the effort was too much for him and he collapsed again. The Japanese forced his comrades to continue with the gruesome work of burying the man. In another instance, a detail of Americans was ordered to dig a trench and bury ten sick Filipinos. One of the Filipinos, already half-covered with earth, sat up, fell back again, was covered with dirt, sat up again, fell back, and was again covered. When he sat up for the third time, a Japanese guard bayoneted him in the face.

In all these instances, the prisoners who were forced to participate could only protest feebly at the inhumanity of the Japanese. Too much of a protest might easily bring their own death. Indeed, hunger, disease, and captivity had reduced them to such a numbed state that even the burying alive of a fellow man brought no more than a temporary shock of revulsion. Later, the full horror of what they had been forced to do would come back to haunt some of the men.

Whether a prisoner was a general or a private made little difference at Balanga. Indeed, it might go harder with the general. Brigadier General Clifford Bluemel and several other officers arrived by truck on April 15th. A Japanese sergeant questioned them through an interpreter. When he discovered Bluemel's rank, he suddenly became excited, almost hysterical, shouting *"Shosho! Shosho!"* ("General! General!"). He drew his sword and struck Bluemel on the head with great force. Fortunately, he hit him with the broad edge of it. The general went down with a gash in his head, hurt but far from dead. Then the sergeant began to beat the other officers. In another part of Balanga, a Japanese officer beat Brigadier General Maxon Lough with a wooden club, but he too managed to survive.

Despite the grisly sights and fetid smells of Balanga, the halt here was usually a welcome one for the prisoners. For one thing, it allowed many of them to quench the nagging thirst that had assailed them since the march began. Those in one group were able to drink from an artesian well located within their assigned plot of ground, but others had only the polluted, disease-laden water found in the ditches beside the road. Still another group was permitted the luxury of a bath in the shallow Talisay River. And in the usual inconsistent manner of the Japanese, some guards refused the prisoners in their charge any water at all.

Those men who still had canteens attempted to fill them. A squad of Japanese soldiers entered one compound shouting and waving their arms and took all the canteens at bayonet point. When they saw a man with a canteen, they made a grab for it, and if he protested he was threatened with a gleaming bayonet or was struck with a rifle butt. The Japanese tied the canteens together with a long cord strung through the canteen chains. If a canteen had no chain, they would throw it back on the ground. Some enterprising prisoners had sufficient strength to break the chains off their canteens, and then to retrieve them after they had been discarded by the Japanese. Those without canteens used tin cans or hollow lengths of bamboo to carry their drinking water.

A group of several hundred Americans who still had their canteens were not permitted to fill them. But a Japanese guard with a head for business was doing very well. For a ring or a watch or some other item he would take a man's canteen, fill it with water, and return it to him. Then he would quickly look around for the next bidder for his service. Many of the prisoners got water that way, and the Japanese guard ended up with enough merchandise to open a small jewelry store.

A few prisoners tried to alleviate their thirst by chewing the moisture from the soft inside of nearby banana trees. But the taste was so bitter that instead of easing the dryness it only increased it.

Meals for the hungry prisoners were fuller and more frequent once the men reached Balanga. But no one grew fat on the diet, and some continued to starve. The Japanese had planned to feed the captives for the first time at this point. Perhaps food handed out in southern Bataan came from stocks originally earmarked for issue here but, whatever the reason, many of the prisoners were not fed at all at Balanga. Some of the men were told there would be food to eat, and the news itself was a revitalizing stimulus to the famished troops. But when such assurances were given, they were not always honored.

The Japanese announced to one group of Americans that they would be fed. But when a search of the prisoners revealed that one colonel had hidden a pistol in his pack, the hungry men were lined up and marched out again without any food. After hiking half the night to the town of Orani, the prisoners were finally allowed to rest their weary bodies. It was the middle of the morning before they received anything to eat—about half a cup of dry rice and some salt.

About 400 Americans who had been with General Bluemel

on the last II Corps line had been promised food several times on their march up the East Road. Yet each time they had been disappointed. Finally at Balanga, Major Thomas J. H. Trapnell, the senior officer in the group, decided to do something about the situation. He caught the attention of some of the Japanese, told them forcefully that his men were exhausted and starving, and demanded food for them. Surprisingly enough, his bold stand paid off. The Japanese gave each man a large serving of rice and a big piece of rock salt. Captain Fred Yeager, knowing how badly he needed the salt, combined it with his rice and then discovered that the mixture was unpalatable. He forced himself to swallow it anyway.

None of those who ate at Balanga dined royally. Usually the only meal they had consisted of a single rice ball, and occasionally the rice had turned sour before the hungry prisoners received it. Rice, ironically enough, would have been an appropriate food for the men suffering with dysentery, who were limited in what they could eat with safety. Yet under the circumstances the amount issued was so small that the danger of starvation was as great as that of succumbing to dysentery. Even then, the lips of some of the men were so blistered from the sun that they could barely eat.

Outside of one compound the Japanese were cooking steaming cauldrons of rice and sausage. The tempting aroma drifted across to the hungry prisoners and drove them almost frantic. But the meal was for the Japanese only.

Some of the captured men were allowed to buy rice from the Filipino civilians who had returned to Balanga. But no fires were permitted, and the prisoners could not cook the rice. In desperation, the men held the raw rice in their mouths until it was soft enough to swallow. Two Filipinos who tried to cook their rice were forced to dig their own graves and then were buried alive. They were not even given a coup de grâce with a shovel or bayonet—just buried.

A few of the prisoners sitting in one field managed to root up some native turnips missed in the last harvest. The vegetables were small but tasty, and the men searched for them with diligence and avidity.

Some of the captives fortunate enough to get some food from the Japanese received it immediately on their arrival at Balanga. But usually the rice was issued to the men as they left. Japanese soldiers with large wooden drums or fifty-gallon cans of rice stood alongside the road above the town. As each prisoner passed, a portion of cooked rice and a little salt was hurriedly dropped into his canteen cup or, if he had none, his outstretched hands. Sometimes all the rice was distributed before a column of prisoners had completely passed the issuing point, and then the men in the rear went hungry. The captives were not permitted to stop and eat the precious rice, but had to wolf it down as they marched.

For the movement north from Balanga, the Japanese organized the prisoners into groups of 100, usually formed into four columns, with a Filipino or American officer at the head of each unit. The marching men were segregated, Americans in one group, Filipinos in another. For the first time, the evacuation of the Luzon Force troops had some semblance of military order, although the men who painfully dragged themselves up the road from Balanga looked more like scarecrows than soldiers.

In contrast to the march below Balanga, when many of the prisoners walked unguarded, each unit of 100 captives had at least one Japanese guard, and sometimes as many as ten. These guards were placed at intervals alongside each group. With fixed bayonets, they prodded the captives along, shouting orders and gesticulating, and kept the columns well closed up. As before, anyone who lagged in sight of a guard felt a bayonet or rifle butt in his ribs.

The great number of prisoners leaving Balanga daily in long, orderly lines contrasted strongly with the scattered, disorganized groups that had straggled into the town. Major Salvador T. Villa recalled that there seemed to be "one continuous column" marching up the road. As he looked back after several hours, there were prisoners "as far as one could see all the way from Balanga."

13

"Another Corpse, Beside the Road"

From Balanga, General Kawane had hoped to use trucks or other vehicles to transport as many of the prisoners as he could—perhaps as many as 25 per cent of them—out of Bataan. The more prisoners who traveled by motor, the sooner Bataan would be cleared for the forthcoming attack on Corregidor, the happier General Homma would be, and the sooner Kawane would be freed of a rather troublesome responsibility. Moving so many of the captives by vehicle would also, of course, make things a lot easier for the exhausted men. But whether Kawane's motives were practical or humanitarian, a great many Americans and Filipinos did begin the movement north from Balanga in trucks or buses.

How many of the prisoners were actually able to ride out of Bataan is difficult to say. Like all statistics about the Death March, the figures are hardly better than educated guesses. Certainly a large number of the captives did not have to walk. This is clear. After the war, many of the former prisoners described how they rode in trucks or buses from Balanga, or told of seeing others who did the same. As one Japanese soldier then in San Fernando wrote in his diary shortly after the surrender, "There were lots of trucks returning loaded with prisoners."

The 14th Army estimate that a maximum of one-fourth of the captured men would be able to ride was based on an anticipated total of about 40,000 prisoners. This meant that transportation for at most 10,000 men might be available. Unless the Japanese were able to exceed this—which seems doubtful—and even if they squeezed more prisoners into each vehicle than comfort or safety allowed—which seems more likely—this is probably the maximum acceptable figure.

There is sufficient evidence from American, Filipino, and Japanese witnesses to support an estimate of several thousand riders. One bit of corroboration comes from Susumu Sato, a Japanese veteran of Bataan who had fought there with the 65th Brigade. Captured later in the war, he was questioned about his knowledge of the Death March. It was his recollection that on each of the five days from April 14th through the 18th he had seen roughly 200 trucks carrying about thirty-five prisoners apiece moving north from Balanga. This would make for a total of approximately 35,000 riders.

Given the normal fallibilities of memory and the understandable tendency to exaggerate, this is obviously much too high. But since Sato made his statement during a routine prisoner of war interrogation rather than in a War Crimes trial where his own or someone else's life was at stake, his testimony cannot be ignored. When combined with other evidence, it certainly indicates that the Japanese provided transportation for a substantial number of Filipinos and Americans.

Between Balanga and San Fernando, where the prisoners would board trains, the Japanese had planned halts at the towns of Orani and Lubao. With a few exceptions this plan was followed. Some of the men did not stop at Orani, but made their first halt at Lubao. Others went past one or both of these towns, or rested at them for only a few hours, but made stops at other towns along the route. Many of the captives were halted for rest or food at a number of small towns as well as at the two main stopping points. At Dinalupihan, midway on the journey, where a few of the prisoners spent the night, some of the senior officers were well fed. They ate rice, fish and meat stew, and, as one of them recalled, "plenty of sugar." They were also allowed to bathe and to wash their filthy clothes.

The 400 Americans in Major Trapnell's group boarded Japanese trucks at Balanga and rode all the way to Camp O'Donnell without stopping. A large group of Filipinos did the same, with a single halt at Dinalupihan. One column of about 600 prisoners marched along with a company of the 65th Brigade, then hiking out of Bataan along the East Road. About three miles above Orani, the captured men were placed in trucks. They rode the rest of the way to San Fernando. Other prisoners walked only as far as Orani before they were ordered onto trucks or buses. Some rode only the first lap of the trip, from Balanga to Orani, others only the final stage, from Lubao to San Fernando. About forty Americans at a makeshift aid station at Balanga were unable to walk. Japanese trucks took them to San Fernando.

The tragic story of the movement from Balanga to O'Donnell is not to be found in an account of those thousands of fortunate men who traveled in trucks or buses, for they suffered relatively little or not at all. Rather it is in the odyssey of that great mass of prisoners who stumbled their pathetic way on foot up the dusty road out of Bataan. It was on these men that four months of half-rations and their attendant malnutrition and disease had their inevitable effect. Japanese brutality and indifference continued unabated, but now there were other horrors. In their first days of captivity, the men of the Luzon Force had suffered more from Japanese cruelty than from their own physical debilities. Yet on the sun-baked road above Balanga, exhaustion and dread disease were almost as punishing.

Already enervated by malnutrition, most of the prisoners were further weakened by malaria. This scourge of the tropics alternately chilled and fevered its victims, leaving them shaken and exhausted. Beneath the burning Philippine sun the sick men shook with cold or writhed with fever, perspiring heavily and losing water that their rapidly dehydrating bodies could not spare.

Dysentery also tortured the captives. The incidence of dysentery had been high enough during the fight for Bataan. Its spread after General King's surrender was hastened even further by the universal thirst that gripped the prisoners and made them drink polluted water against their better judgment. Not quite so widespread as malaria, dysentery was more readily apparent because of its cruel symptoms.

Sores formed on the walls of the sick men's intestines, turning their bowels into a mess of festering corruption. In most cases dysentery victims suffered from diarrhea, and their stool became a horrible mixture of water, fecal matter, blood and mucus.

Losing water and suffering high temperatures in the blazing heat, the men often fell into an extreme lassitude. From this torpor, in the absence of proper medical care, death was at times the only release. In those prisoners already suffering from malnutrition and malaria, dysentery frequently induced a state of such complete weariness, debility, and apathy as to drain from them their last drops of energy and will.

The routine of the march itself was, with a few exceptions, no different from what it had been below Balanga. The days were as hot, the sun as ruthless, the Japanese guards as brutal and indifferent as before. Aside from overnight halts, stops for water were brief and infrequent. Sometimes the Japanese refused them altogether and kept the thirsty men away from wells or pools of water by force. Prisoners who could stand their thirst no longer and broke ranks to get some water were beaten, shot, or bayoneted.

The sick and dehydrated captives drank any water they could, no matter how obviously polluted it was. As disease spread, thirst increased until it became unbearable. The risk of being killed by a Japanese guard was ignored if there seemed to be a chance of getting water. A group of men were halted agonizingly close to a dripping waterpipe above Orani. Colonels Virgil N. Cordero and Alexander Campbell both made a dash for it. Cordero succeeded in getting some water, but a Japanese guard bayoneted Campbell in the leg.

Some men were so thirsty, so sick, so tired that the thrust of a bayonet seemed a welcome relief. A few even begged the Japanese guards to kill them. In their pain-drugged torpor, they had lost the will to live. Surrounded by enemies, they looked at death and thought they saw a friend.

One group of prisoners became separated from the rest of their column below Orani and sat down on the road. Before the arrival of Japanese guards could interfere, some Filipino civilians managed to bring the parched captives enough buckets of water to satisfy their thirst. Almost hysterical in their relief, the men chuckled to themselves as they realized that they had been able to drink all they wanted despite the Japanese. In this, at least, they had defeated their captors and they felt a tremendous surge of pleasure. Even after they were herded to their feet and set to marching again, they continued to re-enact over and over again in their minds how they had enjoyed the water and outwitted their guards.

As the long, ragged columns of prisoners stumbled on through the scorched, dry oven of northern Bataan and pushed into central Luzon, they encountered more and more Filipino civilians. These Filipinos lined the dusty road in silence, their eyes expressing mute sympathy at the piteous procession. Whenever they could do so without endangering their own lives—and frequently despite the danger—the civilians passed food, water, and cigarettes to the staggering men. Bread, rice cookies, lumps of sugar or cane, candy, fruits, hardboiled eggs, bananas, and anything else that could be hurriedly gathered up were thrown or handed to the captives. Several brave Filipinos gave the "V" sign as the columns of prisoners marched by.

Some of the less altruistic civilians had a lucrative business selling food to those captives who still had any money left. But it was dangerous commerce. A few of the Japanese guards allowed the civilians to give or sell to the marchers. Most forbade it. A number of Filipinos were killed or badly mistreated for their efforts.

To the exhausted and starving prisoners, the food was like manna from heaven. And even more uplifting to their spirits was the fact that this food represented a gesture of kindness, a human trait that the tortured men thought had disappeared from the face of the earth. They tried to express their thanks and appreciation to the Filipino civilians, but most were incapable of more than a few muttered words.

Despite the courage and kindness of the civilians, not many prisoners were able to get enough food from them to satisfy their appetites. Yet even a tiny piece of sugar seemed to give new life to a man. One American paid three pesos for a little fruit and rice. It "was worth millions to me," he recalled.

For the sick and rapidly tiring prisoners, halts for rest or food were often confused affairs. Frequently the signal to stop would be misinterpreted for a sign to move to the rear. When the prisoners started to move back, the Japanese guard behind the column would halt them and send them forward again. Thus, instead of resting, the men would spend their time moving back and forth, or just milling around. Often, when a halt was called, the men in front would walk off the road in search of water and those in the rear would continue marching, either because they did not realize that the column was supposed to stop or in the hope of getting some water themselves.

The Japanese continued to kill many stragglers who were too weak to maintain the pace of the march. Time after time, men who were sick or simply tired were shot, bayoneted, beheaded, or beaten to death. The ditches alongside the road were filled with bodies, mute and tragic warnings to the prisoners still marching of the fate awaiting them if they should falter.

Master Sergeant James Baldasarre was walking beside an American colonel who was keeping up only with great difficulty. Suddenly, just below Orani, the colonel broke off from the line of march and started toward a house beside the road. When Baldasarre called after him, the other replied, "I can't make the hike anymore. My feet hurt me." "You'll be shot!" yelled Baldasarre. "I have to take that chance," answered the colonel. Those were his last words. A Japanese guard raised his rifle and pulled the trigger. His bullet struck the colonel in the back.

Another prisoner, a Filipino, unable to keep up with a column of his compatriots, had fallen back to a group of Americans. The American prisoners shouted to the Filipino: "Joe, get up there! Hurry up! Here comes a Jap guard!" But the Filipino, already half out of his mind from suffering, ignored these warnings and wandered out of the American column to the side of the road. Suddenly he saw a pool of water, dashed forward, and threw himself face down into it. A Japanese guard ran over and kicked him several times. When the Filipino failed to get up, or even move, the Japanese plunged his bayonet between the man's shoulder blades. The Filipino made a noise like a baby crying and collapsed. The guard placed his foot on the body, jerked out his bayonet, and rejoined the column of prisoners.

To see men die like this was no longer strange to the captives. It would be wrong to say that they became accustomed to these brutalities, but certainly the initial shock and surprise were gone. The blistering heat of the day, the torpor and apathy induced by disease, the very effort required to maintain life made men almost indifferent to the fate of their companions. Death was commonplace and staying alive more important than anything else.

The blunted feelings of the men toward their fallen comrades were perhaps best expressed in these lines that Lieutenant Henry G. Lee, an American soldier-poet who himself would die while a prisoner of the Japanese, wrote about the death of a friend:

> So you are dead. The easy words contain
> No sense of loss, no sorrow, no despair.
> Thus hunger, thirst, fatigue, combine to drain
> All feeling from our hearts. The endless glare,
> The brutal heat, anesthetize the mind.
> I cannot mourn you now. I lift my load,
> The suffering column moves. I leave behind
> Only another corpse, beside the road.

14

Out of Bataan

As the weary columns of prisoners approached Orani, the men were suddenly aware of a nauseating, pervasive stench. It struck the nostrils like a disgusting gas, penetrating the senses of even those whose minds and bodies had been all but numbed by exhaustion and disease. The closer the captives came to the Orani assembly area, the more powerful and overwhelming became the smell. Soon the cause of it was evident. More and more of the prisoners were coming down with dysentery in its most horrible form, and as they reached and passed through Orani in growing numbers most of the camp site became fouled with diseased human excrement.

The bewildered prisoners stumbled into the ugly, stinking town to find that much of it, like Balanga, was all but razed to the ground. Japanese guards hurried the captives into a small field completely surrounded with barbed wire. Some of the men thought it was a cattle stockade, still filthy with the refuse of the animals. Kicks and bayonets prodded any laggards. Once inside the enclosure, the men found themselves crowded together in an area so packed with their fellow prisoners that any thought of rest quickly vanished. There was simply no room to lie down or even stretch out a bit. Instead, the men were forced to squat or sit, back to back or knee to knee. A hedge divided the compound in two, separating Americans from Filipinos. But in the crowded enclosure, many on both sides broke through the hedge, seeking more room for themselves.

And over everything hung the sickening smell. The only provision made for those who had to relieve themselves was a straddle trench, an open ditch dug in one corner of the field. Even under the best of circumstances, this is far from a sanitary means of disposing of human waste. At Orani, the straddle trench and the area around it was a mass of wriggling maggots. It seemed to many of the prisoners that the earth itself was alive and moving, and so ugly was the sight that none dared approach it. Only because the men had little in their stomachs were they able to avoid vomiting. But few were not sickened. The captives squatted helplessly on the corrupt and stinking ground, often next to a putrifying body. Dysentery victims continued to befoul themselves and the ground around them, and the disease spread rapidly and unchecked.

Orani was the first major halt for most of the captives who made the torturous journey on foot from Balanga to San Fernando. The bulk of these men remained here only overnight, but some stayed twenty-four hours. Treatment was generally the same for all of them, though, and varied only slightly from group to group and individual to individual.

The Japanese gave a single small serving of dry rice and salt to most of the prisoners. Those who stayed longer received two. As usual, a few of the men found themselves out of luck when the rice being issued to their group ran out before all could be served. Those who by one means or another had managed to retain some food of their own were permitted to eat it unmolested.

A few men in one group even managed to climb a mango tree just outside the enclosure and secure some of its fruit. But then there was a shot, and the prisoners in the compound heard a body fall heavily to the ground. No one else in the group went after mangoes.

Near the assembly area was an artesian well with a single spigot, from which the Japanese allowed most of the prisoners to get a little water and sometimes even fill their canteens, if they had any. The thirsty men crowded around the faucet, shoving and elbowing each other for a chance at the precious fluid. Often all they could get was just half a cup.

A group of parched Filipinos pushed close to the well in growing confusion, fighting for a chance at the water. As the milling men became more unruly, several Japanese soldiers moved in amongst them in an attempt to restore order. At first they were unnoticed by many of the prisoners, who were intent on getting to the water, and an anxious Filipino accidentally elbowed one of the Japanese. In a moment, he was rudely yanked from the group around the faucet and tied roughly to a tree.

The Japanese soldier who had been pushed raised his rifle

and fired, striking the Filipino high on the shoulder. Slowly, almost leisurely, he aimed and fired again. This time he missed his target altogether, as he did with a third shot. The wounded Filipino, eyes wide with fear and pain, watched helplessly as the Japanese carefully leaned his rifle against a barrel, lit a cigarette, and then walked unhurriedly over to the faucet for a drink. After quenching his thirst he picked up his rifle, attached the bayonet, and returned to his victim. Suddenly he lunged. The Filipino let out a loud "u-u-mph!" as the bayonet went into his body just below his heart. A second lunge hit him higher in the chest and, as he slumped in his bonds, a third struck him in the groin. The Japanese pulled out the Filipino's shirttail, carefully wiped his bayonet, replaced it in its scabbard, and walked away.

In contrast to this gruesome incident, most of the prisoners were not molested by the Japanese at Orani. There was no looting, apparently, and very little physical mistreatment. And in general the Filipinos and Americans were left more or less to themselves.

Heat, hunger, exhaustion, and disease took their toll nevertheless. "The sun was ruthless," recalls Colonel Ray M. O'Day. Some of the men held shelter halves over their heads and huddled together, trying to rest or sleep. But the blazing heat claimed its victims and a few fell into a delirium from which they never escaped.

When the sickened captives rose from the filth and stench of Orani to move on again, they left behind them on the stained and diseased ground the ugly forms of comrades who would march no more. The Japanese buried some of these unfortunates, caring little, as usual, whether or not the men were still alive. One Filipino "corpse" suddenly reached up from his grave and pulled a Japanese guard in with him. The guard jerked himself free, leaped back, and then bayoneted the Filipino in the head.

Many of the bodies remained where they lay until after the last Japanese had left Orani. Then the Filipino inhabitants of the town pushed the putrifying remains into an abandoned well, covered them with leaves, and set the funeral pyre ablaze.

Above Orani, the Death March continued in the merciless heat. There were no trees to offer shade or cover from the burning sun, and in the flat, open countryside its shimmering rays were harshly reflected from the hard-baked earth into the prisoners' eyes. The air was still and breathless.

Thirst was a steady plague, a dry torture from which the men constantly sought relief. A few who had managed to get mangoes at Orani chewed the thick rind and juicy pulp as they walked, trying to extract the last drop of moisture from the fruit. Others, less fortunate, braved the wrath of the Japanese guards to drink from pools of polluted water, often unmindful of bloated human carcasses floating before them. Sometimes an exhausted captive would put his head to a ditch to drink and never rise again.

On April 12th, one very long column of Americans, perhaps a thousand men altogether, marched all the way from Orani to San Fernando with only an occasional brief halt to change guards or to let Japanese troops go by, and with one two-hour rest at Lubao. During this trek, the only physical mistreatment came at the hands of Japanese soldiers who searched and looted the men from time to time. More punishing, however, was the lack of food and water. The hungry prisoners, many of whom had eaten only a little rice in the three days since King's surrender, received no food whatsoever. The only water they had came in small amounts from the artesian wells that lined the road. As the column moved past each well, the men held canteen cups or other containers under the faucet, and in this manner managed to get a little water to ease their thirst. But the Japanese would allow no one to halt and fill his canteen. Any such intentions were quickly discouraged.

In other groups, hunger and thirst became so great that the men no longer cared what happened to them. In one column, several desperate prisoners suddenly left the road during a halt and started across an open area toward a field of sugar cane. Oblivious to the rifle fire from the Japanese guards—which fortunately was none too accurate—the men frantically broke off stalks of cane and returned with them to the column. As they resumed the march, they stripped the bark from the cane with their teeth and chewed the pulp to extract its sustaining juice—a primitive but excellent way of getting both food and water. Lieutenant Colonel Raymond M. Williams, an American medical officer marching with this group, was convinced "that this simple expedient saved the lives of many men on that day's march." Yet, significantly, these men were so exhausted and apathetic that none had tried to escape when he had the chance.

By now many of the captives had great blisters on the bottom of their feet. As the skin tore off their soles and heels under the constant pressure, the searing pain became almost unbearable. The road in northern Bataan was torn up and full of holes from the heavy shelling of four months of battle, and the prisoners stumbled along with difficulty. Some of the men threw away their shoes and wound pieces of blanket around their feet. Only the thought of their families and the determination to see them again kept others going.

Alongside the road were the still bodies of their comrades who had been unable to keep up. Some had been obviously bayoneted or shot. Many were headless. In fascinated horror, one American officer began counting the corpses of victims who had been beheaded. But as his count neared thirty he started to fear for his sanity and abruptly ended his macabre tally.

Another officer, an older man, could not regain his feet with the others after a rest period. When he finally managed to stand, the rest of the column was some distance ahead of him. As he plodded doggedly after them, a Japanese guard motioned him to catch up with the rest of the prisoners. The officer tried to run but the attempt was too much and he fell flat on his face. With a great effort, he stood up and again tried to run. Once more he fell, but this time he could not rise. Slowly rolling over onto his back, he lay helpless on the ground. The Japanese guard ran up and plunged his bayonet into the prostrate officer.

Many fallen prisoners were beaten to death by their brutal captors. Captain Al Poweleit, a husky American doctor, could stand it no longer when he saw a lone Japanese clubbing an exhausted enlisted man. A former semiprofessional boxer, Poweleit stepped between the two and knocked the guard down with a right to the jaw. Then he leaped on the Japanese, twisted his head until he heard the neck snap, and threw the body into a bamboo thicket beside the road. Fortunately, no other guards had been near enough to witness the scene. Poweleit quickly helped the enlisted man to his feet, and the two rejoined the other marchers.

As the long columns of prisoners pushed grimly along through the last miles of northern Bataan, truckloads of Japanese soldiers headed south continued to pass them. One of them swung his bayoneted rifle at Captain Bert Bank as he rode by him. Bank ducked, but the sharp edge of the bayonet struck a Filipino marching behind him and almost completely took the man's head off. Hardly had Bank recovered from this shocking experience when a sedan pulled up beside him. A Japanese officer in the rear seat waved his arm at him and began barking questions in Japanese. Bank shook his head to indicate that he could not understand what the Japanese was saying. This seemed to enrage his questioner. He hit the American several times, then pushed him back into the column and drove off again.

An American colonel was marching on the inside of the road, an easy target for passing Japanese who continually struck at him with rifle butts and bamboo poles. Colonel Pembroke A. Brawner volunteered to change places with his unfortunate comrade, but it was too late. One blow in particular seemed to have had a telling effect, and the injured colonel soon fell to the rear of the column and collapsed. Three other American officers picked him up and were half carrying, half dragging him along when a guard forced them to drop their burden in the dust. The colonel lay on the road until a Japanese bayonet ended his suffering.

Generals Bluemel and Stevens were leading a group of

American soldiers up the northern end of the East Road. The stars that showed their rank caught the attention of some Japanese soldiers passing in a truck. One of the Japanese reached out as he went by and hit Stevens sharply on the head with a bamboo pole, knocking off the general's glasses and sending him reeling in dizzy pain. The stunned officer stumbled to the side of the road, with the worried Bluemel accompanying him. Both men had seen too many examples of what happened to prisoners who fell out, and Bluemel tried to help his friend recover his senses. As the two sat talking, a Japanese guard ran up, pointed a pistol at Bluemel, and forced him back into the column. Then he turned to General Stevens. Still groggy from the blow, Stevens had not yet been able to rise, but finally, prodded by the guard's threats, he managed to regain his feet. For some reason the Japanese let him wander off into a rice field beside the road. Stevens quickly hid himself in a ditch and lay there as the rest of the prisoners went on. Sometime later, when he had regained his strength, he joined another passing column.

Bluemel, meanwhile, had no idea of what had happened to Stevens after he went into the rice field. He himself was nearly felled a little later by a Japanese rifle butt when he stopped to get some water. It was not until Bluemel had been at Camp O'Donnell for three days that Stevens finally arrived to ease his friend's concern.

From Orani to Lubao, the next major step for the marchers, was about fifteen miles, the longest stretch between halting points north of Balanga. As the prisoners left Bataan's East Road and began to push up Route 7, they entered central Luzon for the first time in more than four months. Not since early January, when General MacArthur led them into Bataan, had they been this far north.

The contrast was striking. In January, they were in the midst of a great withdrawal. But they had not been defeated. They were falling back before superior forces, but they were not hungry, sick, and exhausted. And their spirits were high. Now they were a beaten army. What was once a unified, co-ordinated fighting force had become a disorganized mob of weary, starving, dirty, dying men. Gone was their strength, dead was their spirit. Only the will to live kept them marching.

If conditions at Orani were bad, those at Lubao were worse. At the entrance to the town, Filipinos lined the road and tossed food to the prisoners or passed them cans of water. Some of the Filipino prisoners even managed to slip into the crowd and make good their escape by pretending to be civilian residents of Lubao. A few Americans were equally successful.

But once the prisoners had passed the crowd of welcoming Filipinos, the situation changed rapidly. To the right of the road, they saw a large fenced-in area, perhaps 300 feet long and half as wide. In the center of this enclosure was a sheet-iron warehouse, with a concrete floor, about 150 by 70 feet in size. This building was a warehouse of the National Rice and Corn Corporation, but it was to be used for a purpose that the company had never envisioned. At first the prisoners were allowed to sit outside in the yard but, as that area grew more and more crowded, the men were driven inside, first by the urge to find room in which to stretch out and then, when they hesitated, by the bayonets of the guards.

Those who remained outside the warehouse were fortunate—but only by comparison. Sanitary conditions here were the worst that any of the prisoners had yet encountered, and the noxious odor of human refuse hung heavily over the area. Dysentery stools covered the ground. Rotting corpses dotted the yard. Mosquitoes and other insects constantly plagued the men. A few straddle trenches had been dug, but not many prisoners had the fortitude to use them. Only the dying were not bothered by the overpowering stench.

In one corner of the yard, in the shade of a large tree, a small area had been set aside for the very sick. Three American medical officers were trying to assist the many prisoners who lay on the ground here. The Japanese had ordered anyone with medicine to turn it in at this improvised aid station, but only a handful of drugs could be found. For the most part, the three doctors could only comfort their patients and watch helplessly as the weaker men died.

On the other side of the yard was a single water faucet. A long line of thirsty captives stood waiting before it under the watchful eye of a Japanese sentry. From the faucet the water dripped down in a thin, tantalizing stream. The line moved agonizingly slowly and some men, with a patience born of desperation, waited hours for their turn at the precious water. Each carried a canteen or bucket for himself, and two or three others for friends too sick to stand in line. Prisoners who attempted to break ahead of someone else or to rush the spigot were knocked down and sometimes killed by the guard. And when a Filipino and an American got into an argument in front of the faucet, the Japanese shot them both.

Most of the men were silent. Only their eyes betrayed

their great thirst. But years later one officer could still hear the horrifying sound made by the continuous clinking of the canteens, hour after hour, day after day, frightening in its deadly monotony, as the prisoners stood patiently waiting their turn.

Inside the warehouse was another spigot. But only those lucky enough to be next to it could use it. There were too many other men, jammed so closely together that they were unable to move, for anyone else to get near the faucet. Only the men around it, of all of the thousands of captives at Lubao, were able to drink their fill of water.

The prisoners were packed inside the warehouse until there was barely room to sit down. The guards, with fixed bayonets, kept pressing more and more men into the building, jamming those already inside tighter and tighter against each other. Then they closed the doors. Within the warehouse, lying down or stretching out in any manner was out of the question. A few of the men did manage to lie on top of each other, the only way they could rest, but many prisoners could do nothing but stand. Some of the men in the building later estimated that there may have been several thousand captives squeezed into the warehouse at once.

The inside of the building was filthy with the refuse of the many dysentery victims. The doors and windows were closed, and the air soon became putrid with the heavy odor of unwashed bodies and diseased human feces. A few cracks in the wall provided the only ventilation in the building, hardly enough to matter. The smell of the dead was also there. But when General Stevens, who was among those pressed into the warehouse, requested that the bodies be removed, he was given a curt refusal.

In the crowded, unsanitary conditions, the dysentery spread rapidly. Nobody could sleep and the dark was filled with moaning and cursing. Men leaned on each other or trampled on one another. Where at first the prisoners had sought to sit down and rest, now they fought to stay erect and live. For when a man went down, he did not always arise. When the sick and exhausted captives were taken from the warehouse in the morning to resume the trip, there remained the still forms of those who could go no further. Most of these men were dead. Some still lived, but they had entered a state of shock combined with disease that would find its only release in death.

The warehouse at Lubao was not as crowded on every night. Sometimes there was even enough room for men to lie on the concrete floor and, with their musette bags as pillows, to get some sleep. For these prisoners, the stop was a welcome rest. The Japanese fed everyone two meals a day of rice and salt and permitted them to eat their own food, if they had any. Again few of the men were allowed to light cooking fires.

Most of the captives remained here only overnight but, as at other stopping points, many stayed longer. For those with road blisters, a halt of two or three days meant the difference between torn and whole skin on their feet, perhaps even between life and death.

But if the rest and food gave some men new strength for the remaining miles, this was more than balanced by the many who died in the crowded warehouse, who were killed by brutal Japanese guards, or who succumbed to exhaustion and disease. There were few survivors who did not look back on the stop at Lubao as the worst, the most horrible night they had ever spent.

15

San Fernando

Eight miles northeast of Lubao was San Fernando, the largest town on the route of march, an important rail and road hub, and the capital of Pampanga Province. Touched only lightly by the swift passage of battle, it had a fair-sized Filipino population, and many homes, schools, factories, and other buildings. A "beehive of Japanese hordes," in the words of one Filipino, had also descended on the town, and soldiers were constantly moving through its streets. For the captured men of the Luzon Force, growing weaker each day, San Fernando was the beginning of the final stage of their tragic exodus from Bataan.

The first large groups of prisoners reached San Fernando on April 11th, two days after the surrender. Riding in trucks, they seemed worn, hungry, and tired to the townspeople. But their spirits were firm and they held their heads high. For the next two days, prisoners continued to arrive by truck. It was not until April 13th that the first of the many thousands of captives moving on foot reached San Fernando. For two weeks the prisoners poured into the town in great numbers, and even after that smaller groups continued to trickle in.

The march from Lubao to San Fernando, while relatively short, was still a nightmare for most of the men. Hurried along by the Japanese in the burning sun, even the strongest weakened and fell. Tanks and trucks had chewed up the road, forcing the captives to pick their way gingerly, seeking the best footing. The hot, sticky asphalt burnt the soles of those with tattered footgear, or with no shoes at all. Japanese soldiers riding by in trucks continued to lean out and club the prisoners as they went by. Just before reaching San Fernando the captives had to pass in single file before several of these trucks, parked so that they almost blocked the road. As the helpless prisoners walked by, they were easy targets for the men in the trucks. Physical exhaustion, the hot sun, and Japanese brutality combined so that some groups of captives lost more men on this day's march than they had on any previous day.

There were no Filipino civilians along the road to greet the first columns. The Japanese had issued orders forbidding anyone to give food or water to the prisoners, and for a few days these orders were obeyed. Then more and more civilians appeared to offer the captives assistance and encouragement. Usually they got away with it, although sometimes the guards fired at them. In a few cases Japanese soldiers chased the Filipinos into fields well off the road and shot them. But the food and water that these brave civilians gave the grateful prisoners often meant the difference between life and death.

Colonel Alexander S. Quintard bought some dirty peanut brittle wrapped in newspaper from a Filipino. "I really believed it saved our lives," he later recalled.

Occasionally the Americans were sickened by the sight of a Filipino who had suddenly forgotten his ties with the United States and had become pro-Japanese. One in particular, still wearing his army uniform, was loudly denouncing the American prisoners to the great amusement of the Japanese soldiers.

All along the road the Japanese continued to beat and kill stragglers. They forced one column of prisoners to double-time the entire distance, allowing the exhausted men a five-minute break each hour. How any of them managed to survive is almost beyond belief, but all understood only too well that it was either double-time or death.

A few miles above Lubao, two American enlisted men in another group collapsed. Fortunately there were no guards nearby, and an American colonel helped the stricken men climb into a Filipino cart standing with its driver beside the road. As he got in himself, some Japanese soldiers came along. One grabbed the whip from the startled driver's hand and began to lay about him with great force. Somehow, the Americans made it back into the line of march, while the Filipino ran off into the fields.

As if the testimony of their eyes was not enough for the prisoners, the Japanese issued some groups a formal printed declaration that anyone attempting to escape would be shot to death. But for many men, especially those who feared they were too weak to continue marching, the risk was well worth the effort. This was especially true of the Filipinos who, if they once got off the road, stood a good chance of mingling with the civilians and escaping. The townspeople along the way did what they could to help them. Some of the Filipino prisoners slipped into culverts under the road and lay in the water until the rest of the captives had passed. Later, under cover of darkness, they walked to the nearest town where they were taken in and hidden.

In one group of Filipinos passing through a town, the stronger men were able to push their weaker comrades into houses standing close to the road. Afraid to stay themselves, lest the absence of too many men be noticed, they asked the nervous civilians to take care of the sick men and to give a decent burial to any who died.

Several thousand Filipinos probably escaped between Lubao and San Fernando. More might have gotten away, but fear and physical weakness kept many of them from trying.

A few Americans also managed to break away from their captors, usually with the help of friendly civilians. One Air Corps enlisted man, who was having trouble keeping up with the march, saw the Japanese shoot two stragglers. "The way I felt," he wrote later, "I knew it wouldn't be long till they were aiming at me, so I looked for a chance to escape." When the column passed through a small town, he slipped behind a nearby house. Like some others, he was able to stay free, thanks to the Filipino civilians who fed and nursed the men and kept them hidden. When the Americans were strong enough, they slipped off into the hills to join the growing bands of Filipino guerrillas that would be a thorn in the Japanese side during the rest of the occupation.

Day after day, the ragged columns stumbled into San Fernando. To the townspeople who lined the streets, the wretched prisoners seemed more tired and hungry with each passing hour. The Filipino civilians gave what food and water they could to the men, sometimes in defiance of the Japanese guards, sometimes at the great risk of life and limb.

As the news spread rapidly to other parts of Luzon that the prisoners were being brought through San Fernando, people came from all over the island in hopes of seeing a relative or friend. For those who had had no word from their men in the army since almost the start of the war, it was a tense moment. They stood anxiously in the street, straining to see if the one they sought was among the prisoners. Sometimes they spotted a husband, father, or son, and then they rushed to his side, almost oblivious of the guards. Even the Japanese were touched by this display, and many either pretended not to see it or sent the civilians away without punishing them.

The daily sight of the walking captives, struggling to keep up, ragged and emaciated, impressed itself indelibly on the minds of the watching Filipinos. Naturally warm and friendly, they gave their sympathy to the prisoners and suffered along with them. At night, they could not sleep as they remembered the haggard faces of the prisoners, their stumbling walk, the way they begged for food. This was an experience that many of the Filipinos would never forget.

Prisoners were everywhere in San Fernando—in large assembly areas, in smaller ones, and grouped along the streets. The two main points of concentration were the municipal cockpit and the building and yard of the local elementary school.

The San Fernando cockpit was in a large shed, open on

the sides, in the center of a broad field. The feet of thousands of men had trampled the ground to dust. Decomposing bodies and human waste covered the area. The few latrines, just open trenches, were overflowing and swarming with maggots and flies. Nor were they always used. The roof of the shed offered some shelter from the sun, but so crowded was the compound that the men sat anywhere, in sun or shade, where they could find room to get off their feet. One group cleared a small area of filth and fecal matter so that they could sit down, but they could not get rid of the foul smell that clung to the ground. The stench of bloated corpses was so bad that several of the officers asked the Japanese to let them remove the bodies and bury them. To the intense relief of everyone, the guards did not object.

Several thousands of prisoners were crowded into the cockpit each day. Frequently they had room to lie down and stretch out, but often they were so crowded they could barely turn over at night. American medical officers set up an aid station, but without any drugs they could do little to help their dying patients.

Conditions in the schoolhouse and the yard around it were similar. More of the prisoners concentrated here seem to have been sick or dying, and those in better shape could hardly move around without stumbling over a sick comrade or befouling themselves with human refuse.

The Japanese had placed barbed wire around the school yard and stationed many guards in the immediate area. During the day, then, they allowed the captives the freedom of the yard. But after dark all the men were herded inside, where they slept, in the words of one Filipino, "packed like tied salted mustard leaves." On one night a prisoner, haunted perhaps by the terror and agony of the march, shrieked aloud in his sleep. His cry shattered the stillness and woke his comrades from their own troubled sleep. A Japanese guard with fixed bayonet rushed into the building to investigate. By now everyone realized what had happened and, seeing the Japanese, as one man they lowered their heads and returned to sleep. The guard looked around for a moment, shrugged his shoulders, and walked out.

Other prisoners, held elsewhere in San Fernando, found themselves in such varied places as the "Blue Moon" dancehall, an old factory, and a pottery shed. Some just waited in the streets or marched directly to the railroad station to board the train for Capas.

Like Lubao and Orani, San Fernando was just an overnight stop for most of the men. But again, as at the other towns, many prisoners remained longer, some for two or three days, a few for more than a week. There was no set pattern, no consistency.

At San Fernando, the Japanese made a definite attempt to feed their captives. They set up large cauldrons for cooking rice, and fed the prisoners twice a day. Most of the men got something to eat this way, although, as usual, there were some who went hungry and others who ate only what they had themselves or what they could get from the townspeople or buy from the guards. Corporal L. Arhutick was particularly fortunate. The Japanese gave his group brown sugar and "all the rice we could eat," and Arhutick, who still had some money, supplemented this by buying chicken, pork, and cigarettes from a Filipino civilian.

At the cockpit, one of the Japanese sentries was doing very well for himself by selling sugar cane to the prisoners. He cut the cane from a nearby field and offered it for two pesos a stalk to any of the men who had been smart or lucky enough to get this far without losing all their currency. "He would have had a flourishing business," recalled one American officer, "had more of us had any money." Why the guard did not simply take the money from the captives is something no one could understand.

There was a single water faucet at the cockpit, and again the men formed long, continuous lines to drink or to fill their canteens. Prisoners elsewhere also received limited amounts of water, and in one area the Japanese allowed the Philippine Red Cross to prepare buckets of limeade for the seriously ill men. In another group of prisoners a Japanese-speaking Filipino officer even managed to talk the Japanese into providing hot coffee for the men.

Some of the captives were able to eat well and get something to drink three times a day, and these men tried to stay at San Fernando as long as they could in order to benefit by this bounty. They did this by slipping away from their own group as it started to leave and attaching themselves to a new body of prisoners just coming in. One American managed to stay in San Fernando for eight days by using this method.

But, sooner or later, all the prisoners had to leave. For the next phase of their trip, none would have to walk. The Japanese had provided trains. Yet so horrible was the ride, that many of the men, had they been able to anticipate it, might well have preferred to march.

16

The Sealed Train

A block or so above the point where Route 7 entered San Fernando from the west was the railroad station. An important stop on the main line from Manila to the north, as well as the junction of two branch lines, the station consisted of several small buildings or sheds and a few sidings for the trains. The prisoners had passed within sight of it as they walked into San Fernando, and most of them returned to it as they left. With the exception of a few men who boarded trucks for the last lap of their journey to Camp O'Donnell, all the captives in the various assembly areas scattered throughout the town were sooner or later marched back to the station. Few would forget it, or the train ride that followed.

The twenty-five-mile trip to the town of Capas might have offered the sick and weary prisoners a chance to rest and recoup some of their strength. But this was not to be. For instead of providing coaches for the men, the Japanese decided to carry them in boxcars normally used for freight. Perhaps this choice was an attempt at preventing escape, since windowless boxcars allowed greater control with fewer guards than did the open coaches. Perhaps it resulted from indifference. Possibly it was dictated by necessity. But whatever the reason, the hearts of the prisoners sank when they reached the San Fernando station and saw the empty boxcars waiting to receive them.

The Philippine railroad system employed the narrow gauge track, so the boxcars at San Fernando were smaller than those in service in the United States. They were of two sizes. The larger, a steel car, was about thirty-three feet long, eight feet across, and seven feet high. The smaller was perhaps half as long, equally wide, a foot less in height, and made of wood. Both had a single door on either side, and this provided the only ventilation other than that allowed by a narrow screened slit at either end of some of the cars.

Even within these rude confines, the prisoners might have been able to make themselves relatively comfortable had the Japanese shown them some compassion. Instead, the captives were packed in so close together that they could hardly move.

With kicks and blows with their rifle butts, the guards drove the harried men into the cars. About one hundred men were jammed into each of the larger ones and about half as many into the smaller. Fortunately, only a few of the latter were used, for in these the taller men found that their heads touched the roof of the car.

The guards used their rifles freely to force more and more prisoners into each car, squeezing the captives so tightly together that no one could change his position once the car was full. If a man sat down, he remained seated, his knees pulled in tightly under his chin. If he was standing, he stood with legs immobile and arms almost helpless for the entire trip.

No sooner were the prisoners inside the cars than most of the doors were slammed shut. The captives managed to open some of them again. When they did, or if the doors were not closed in the first place, the stronger men frequently tried to place their sick comrades by the openings, where they could breathe the fresh air. But in most cases the cars remained sealed while the trains were in motion.

The ride from San Fernando to Capas was the culmination of all the horrors which the prisoners had encountered. Disease, hunger, and brutality had sapped their energy and dissipated their spirits. Now they were exposed to a new and more extreme torture.

Jammed in the dark insides of the boxcars, the men were so crowded that they pressed against each other and fought to breathe the stale air. Worse off than cattle—for cattle are too valuable to be packed so tightly or left with so little ventilation—most of the prisoners fell into a dazed stupor, more dead than alive. Even before the trains jerked to a start, the oppressive heat began to make itself felt, and the men gasped for air in the suffocating atmosphere. As the rolling prisons moved slowly north, the steel sides of the cars grew so hot that they burned the skin of anyone who touched them. Those in the wooden cars escaped this torture, but they had more trouble breathing since there was no room above their heads for the thick air to circulate.

The steel cars quickly became "sweat boxes." Almost the last bit of water in the dehydrated men drained from their protesting bodies in hot beads of unpleasant, sticky perspiration. Each man's sweat was mixed with that of the neighbor who leaned against him. It ran down their legs so profusely that their stockings were soaked and their shoes became soggy.

Dysentery victims had long since ceased trying to control themselves. The refuse of the stricken men covered the floors and filled the closed cars with a stifling and inescapable stench. When the trains halted, the guards sometimes permitted the captives to descend and relieve themselves. More often they did not. In some cases the prisoners themselves segregated their sick comrades at one end of the car in hopes of easing the trip for the others. But it was a futile gesture. The horrible, overpowering smell and the jerky movement of the cars over the rough roadbed made the sick men sicker. Some of them retched and threw up on the already messy floors, on themselves, and on their fellow prisoners.

The nauseating reek grew progressively worse and the heat more oppressive. Many of the men fainted in the suffocating torture chambers. Their bodies slipped to the floor and lay helpless in the filth and slime that covered it. Some did not rise. Others died where they stood, wedged between neighbors whose sensibilities were so numbed that they remained unaware of their comrades' death.

On the average, the men spent about four hours in their boxcar prisons. Many of the captives, their limbs cramped and aching, their minds anesthetized by the heat and the stench, were so dazed that they had no conception at all of the passage of time or the movement of the cars.

The trains traveled slowly, so slowly, in fact, that some of the stronger men standing near open doors were able to leap from the cars to their freedom. Still more opportunities to escape came each time the trains stopped, which they usually did at almost every station between San Fernando and Capas.

At each halt the cars were surrounded by Filipino civilians who showered the prisoners with all sorts of food and drink: tomatoes, bananas, rice, eggs, fried meats, candy, sugar cane, and coffee and water in bottles. Sometimes the Japanese guards drove them back, but then the people would throw their packages into the open car doors. In one car, two guards sat in the open doorway and took their share of the food before allowing any to reach the starving captives. As more and more of the prison trains moved north, the word seemed to spread, and the crowds at the railroad station grew larger every day.

The clothing worn by the Filipino prisoners differed little from that of the onlooking civilians. Some intrepid captives managed to slip out of their cars, tie a rice sack around their waists, and escape by pretending to be local residents. Even if they failed to fool the Japanese, there were so few guards and the crowds were so large that few of these men were recaptured or even pursued.

For the many prisoners who remained, the generosity of the Filipinos in sharing their meager food supplies warmed the hearts of the captives as much as it nourished their bodies. Many a man whose life was saved by their kindness and courage would never forget these friendly people.

When the trains finally reached Capas, the prisoners pushed, shoved, trampled each other, and frequently fell out onto the ground in their haste to escape into the fresh air. Then, blinking their eyes in the harsh glare of the sun and prodded by the guards, they stumbled from the railroad station. Their legs were so stiff from the cramped positions they had been forced to endure that some could hardly stand.

As the men were formed in the usual columns for the final stage of the march to Camp O'Donnell, the Filipino townspeople rushed among them with food and water. A few even gave their hats to prisoners standing bareheaded beneath the burning sun. As usual, some of the guards had no objections; others pushed away the civilians, knocked over baskets of food, and threatened anyone who came near the prisoners. One Filipino captain whose home had been in Capas recognized his brother in the crowd. He quickly passed him his money and several watches that fellow officers had entrusted to him. A few minutes later someone handed the captain a package of food. He looked up and discovered his son standing before him.

When the prisoners began to march west out of Capas, many of them carried in their arms bags of food or bottles of water. A few of the Filipinos, who had formerly lived in Capas, were so refreshed by these provisions and by the sight of home and the welcome of their fellow townspeople, that they were almost cheerful. They marched lightheartedly, feeling better than they had in days.

But the physical condition of most of the prisoners was at its worst. Some were so weak that they could barely lift their feet to walk. All the liquid in their bodies seemed to have been drained from them on the train ride from San Fernando. Some men were sure that no more than a quarter of their number would live to complete the last few miles of the march. Gaunt, haggard, dirty, unshaven, clothes torn and stained with filth, the captives looked at each other unfamiliarly. Even best friends had difficulty recognizing one another.

The shambling columns staggered along the narrow gravel road through green walls of rich foliage. There had been no fighting here, and the beauty of the jungle was untainted save by the presence of the sick, disheveled prisoners. Fortunately the guards did not molest the plodding men. They too, perhaps, were conscious that the end of the march was almost at hand. A few even lent a helping hand to some of the weaker captives. For the most part, they concerned themselves only with preventing stragglers from dropping back.

About a mile from Camp O'Donnell, the stumbling columns topped a rise and saw for the first time the site of their prison. The partially completed Philippine Army post looked crude and uninviting on the dry, rolling, almost treeless plain. Unfinished barracks, some without roofs to turn aside the burning rays of the sun, others with only a bamboo framework holding up a roof of grass, stood naked on the baked and dusty ground. The scorching heat held everything in the fierce oven of the tropical day. Around the camp stood a high barbed-wire fence, broken here and there by wooden sentry towers that rose stark and grim from the arid plain. Thick clumps of tall, still cogon grass seemed to be the only living thing in sight.

The exhausted prisoners staggered through the narrow gates of O'Donnell, wondering mutely what new privations awaited them and, in the words of one Filipino officer, "commending our souls in the hands of Almighty God."

As they painfully stumbled across the hot, dry parade ground of the camp, some of them may have recalled the words of a letter addressed to General Wainwright, copies of which had been dropped by Japanese airplanes all over southern Bataan in March. The letter was sent, it read, "in accordance with the humanitarian principles of 'Bushido,' the code of the Japanese warrior." It urged "honorable surrender" and an end to "needless bloodshed." "International Law will be strictly adhered to by the Imperial Japanese Forces," it declared, "and your Excellency and those under your command will be treated accordingly. The joy and happiness of those whose lives will be saved and the delight and relief of their dear ones and families would be beyond the expression of words."

Those who survived the Death March may well have wondered about "the humanitarian principles of 'Bushido.' "

The arrival of the American and Filipino troops at Camp O'Donnell brought to a close the tragic exodus from Bataan. But their ordeal was far from over, for the horrors of prison camp were no less bitter than those of the Death March.

No sooner had the captives reached O'Donnell than they received a foretaste of what was to come. As each group entered the camp, the Japanese guards counted the prisoners and searched them for weapons, relieving them, in the process, of any trinkets that struck the searchers' fancy. Then the guards marched the men up a small rise to an open area in front of the camp headquarters building. Here the prisoners were told to sit. And here they waited, sometimes as long as several hours in the broiling sun, until at last a Japanese officer came out of the building, strode briskly to a small wooden platform, mounted it, and began to harangue the men.

The officer was a Captain Tsuneyoshi, the camp commandant, and it was his job to greet each new group of prisoners when it reached O'Donnell. And to each group he gave essentially the same fiery speech of welcome—and warning.

Speaking through an interpreter, Tsuneyoshi announced to the prisoners that the Japanese had occupied all Allied possessions in the southwest Pacific, and that they would soon take India and Australia. The United States and Great Britain, he said, were Japan's enemies, and would remain so until the influence of the Occident had been destroyed forever in the Far East. Even if it took one hundred years, Japan would continue to fight, generation after generation, until this had been achieved.

The Americans and Filipinos at O'Donnell, declared Tsuneyoshi, were captives, below the dignity of prisoners of war, eternal enemies of Japan, and completely at his mercy. They owed their lives to the benevolence of the Emperor and the spirit of *Bushido*. Anyone attempting to escape would be shot to death. Anyone who did not obey camp regulations meticulously would be shot to death. All insignia of rank would be removed, and all prisoners would salute all Japanese guards regardless of rank.

Tsuneyoshi did not speak his words. He screamed them. And as he warmed to his oration, his tone became wilder, more angry, more menacing. He thrust his arms forward to emphasize his points, swinging them now horizontally, now vertically. He paused frequently, one arm usually uplifted, while the interpreter translated his words. Then the captain returned to his harangue. He stood slightly bowlegged, his sword dangling at his side and jerking back and forth with the violence of his gestures.

To one group of prisoners that arrived at night, Tsuneyoshi delivered his speech standing atop the hood of a jeep, with the flashlights of the guards trained on him like theatrical spotlights. Watching this spectacle, Captain Paul Krauss was reminded of Charlie Chaplin's impersonation of Hitler in the movie, "The Great Dictator." Indeed, some of the Americans later nicknamed Tsuneyoshi "Little Hitler."

Except for the painful reality of the situation, the effect would have been almost comical. General Jones, for one, standing in line in the first group to be harangued by Tsuneyoshi, could not believe the Japanese officer was serious. The whole thing seemed like a joke to him, and he started to laugh. But General King, who was next to him, dug his elbow into Jones' ribs. "Shut up!" he ordered. And Jones stopped laughing, suddenly realizing that the angry little Japanese officer who stood before him, gesticulating stiffly like some oversized marionette, was not joking at all.

17

The Death Toll

By the early part of May, the Death March was over. Prisoners continued to reach O'Donnell in small numbers for a short time thereafter, but most of the men had arrived in camp within three weeks or a month of General King's surrender.

Just how many captives perished during the tragic evacuation from Bataan is a perplexing question. No accurate answer can be given nor, with the evidence on hand, should a precise reply be attempted. Any estimate at all is little better than a guess.

When the Japanese opened their Good Friday offensive, there were about 78,100 troops in the Luzon Force: an estimated 11,796 Americans and 66,304 Filipinos. But not all of these men participated in the Death March.

Of the total force under General King, about 2,000 men escaped to Corregidor on April 8th or 9th. An additional number, perhaps as many as 4,000, remained as patients or staff in hospitals on Bataan until the end of June. Many prisoners, also, were put to work by the Japanese repairing bridges, driving trucks, and doing other odd jobs, and thus avoided the Death March.

Moreover, many other troops escaped from the line of march or never even surrendered, and made their way unharmed out of Japanese reach. Thousands of Filipinos were able to get away, especially after the groups in which they were walking left Bataan and entered central Luzon. There were also dozens of Americans who hid out in the jungles of Bataan after King's surrender or who broke away to freedom from the marching columns headed toward San Fernando.

The biggest unknown factor in a computation already made difficult by too many unknowns is the number of troops killed in the six days from the start of the Good Friday offensive until General King's surrender.

On this no one has ventured an estimate. Even the official United States Army history of the Philippine campaign is silent. Yet this figure is vital to any attempt at reckoning the number of participants and casualties in the Death March. If many men were killed during the final Japanese attack, then obviously they did not die in the Death March. But if the casualties were few during this attack, then the number of dead chargeable to the Death March will be greater.

Neither American nor Japanese records are of much help in assessing Luzon Force losses from April 3rd through 9th. So great was the disorganization of units under the tremendous pressure of the Good Friday offensive that neither General King nor his subordinate commanders were ever aware of just how many of their men were killed or wounded. Obviously men died. Perhaps many. Colonel Floyd Marshall, King's personnel officer, thought that "the number of killed and wounded was not excessive but that the number of missing was heavy." From the nature of the battle—a heavy artillery and air bombardment, followed by a quick breakthrough and rapid advance with continued artillery and air support—it is probable that casualties were high on the first day or so and moderate thereafter. Whatever the total number of dead, it must be subtracted from the figures for the Death March.

The historian is faced with too many unknown factors—even the figures he has are questionable—to arrive at a reasonable solution.

Looking first at the Americans, of the 11,796 officially estimated to have been on Bataan on April 3rd, at least 1,500 remained in the two hospitals there. About 300 other men are definitely known to have reached Corregidor. Perhaps twenty-five stayed on Bataan to work for the Japanese and an additional fifty or more escaped from the Death March or refused to surrender in the first place. A total of approximately 1,875 men can thus be eliminated from the Death March, almost all of them before the movement began.

Of the estimated 9,921 Americans left unaccounted for, both General King and his personnel officer, Colonel Marshall, stated in their official reports that about 9,300 men reached Camp O'Donnell by the end of May, when most of the American prisoners were transferred elsewhere. Colonel Charles S. Lawrence, the Luzon Force quartermaster, and Colonel Harold W. Glattly, King's medical officer, both men whose duties would concern them with exact strength figures, agree with King and Marshall. Marshall and Lawrence, in fact, have both set the total at 9,271. Subtracting this figure from 9,921, there remain 650 Americans unaccounted for.

These calculations, of course, make no allowance for American deaths during the Good Friday offensive. Since relatively few American soldiers appear to have been killed in this attack, it is probably safe to conclude that between 600 and 650 Americans died in the Death March between southern Bataan and Camp O'Donnell.

The tabulation of Filipino losses is nowhere as certain. From the officially estimated total of 66,304 Philippine Army, Scout, and Constabulary troops on Bataan on April 3rd, we can make one quick deduction with some degree of assurance. Approximately 2,500 Filipino soldiers remained in the Bataan hospitals, perhaps 1,700 escaped to Corregidor, a handful of others were held on Bataan to work for the Japanese—a total of about 4,200 men.

Of the approximately 62,100 Filipinos left unaccounted for, the majority were taken to Camp O'Donnell. But official figures on Filipino arrivals at O'Donnell are nowhere near as certain as they are for the Americans. For one thing, the Japanese separated the Filipino and American troops at the camp and allowed little or no contact between the two groups. So General King and his staff could not calculate with any precision the number of Filipinos imprisoned with them. Also, their estimates do not account for the 26,000 Filipino civilians captured on Bataan. The majority of these men, women, and children were set free by the Japanese, or simply melted away into the hills, but some were undoubtedly killed and a few others were incarcerated with the troops.

But in the absence of any other figures, the rough American estimates must be accepted for whatever they are worth. Colonel Marshall set the figure of Filipino arrivals at Camp O'Donnell at 44,000 men, General King at 45,000, Colonel Lawrence at 46,000 to 48,000, and Colonel Glattly at 50,000. These approximations still leave between 12,000 and 18,000 Filipinos unaccounted for.

What happened to these men is almost impossible to tell. First of all, there is absolutely no record of just how many were killed in the Good Friday offensive, although it is clear that a great number of Filipinos must have lost their lives during this attack. And then, of course, no one knows just how many thousands of Filipinos escaped from the Death March or never surrendered at all.

The only reasonable conclusion is admittedly a guess: between 5,000 and 10,000 Filipinos lost their lives on the Death March. And to this figure add a maximum of 650 American fatalities.

The men who died on the Death March were of all ranks except general, and of every age group. Most of these men were sick and exhausted, but even the stronger ones fell victim to Japanese brutality. Many of the older prisoners were less able to withstand the ravages of disease and starvation than their younger comrades. But some of the younger Americans proved more helpless in the trauma of defeat than did their seniors. To those who had yet to achieve their physical and emotional maturity, General King's surrender was a bitter blow for which they were ill prepared. They could not accept the fact that the Japanese had won, that an American army had actually been defeated.

"They were heartbroken," recalled Colonel Paul Krauss, who himself was then in his early twenties. "This was one time the cavalry didn't come over the hill to the rescue." On top of their already weakened physical condition, the shock of defeat was too much of an added burden for these men. Their will to live was seriously shaken, and the ordeal of the Death March was fatal.

Yet the toll of the exodus from Bataan did not cease when the wretched survivors reached Camp O'Donnell. The troops of the Luzon Force had been starving and sick when they surrendered. The shock of the movement to O'Donnell, the blazing sun, the crowded, fetid assembly areas, the continued lack of nourishment, and the brutality of the guards had drained the last vestiges of strength from their tired bodies and lowered their physical resistance to even the most minor disease. They were, as one man put it simply, "in pitiable condition."

In the hot dusty oven of O'Donnell, with the prisoners still denied sufficient food and medicine and exposed to continued Japanese cruelty and indifference, the effects of the horrible journey from Bataan were grimly evident. In the first six or seven weeks at Camp O'Donnell, more than 1,600 Americans and at least ten times as many Filipinos died. Their deaths were as surely the malignant fruit of the Death March as the rotting corpses that lined the road from Mariveles.

Years later, those who managed to survive could still not erase the nightmare of O'Donnell from their minds. In a conversation recorded in the Pentagon in 1952, on the tenth anniversary of the Death March, General Jones recalled the horrors of the prison camp: "I shall never forget waking at two or three o'clock in the morning with a fog of death laying on the ground and the taste of death in my mouth, and the groans of the dying and the clanging of canteens of columns of Filipinos with bamboos strung between them taking empty canteens dangling and bumping one another on the way to the river to get polluted water, and other columns returning from the river and then, in the daylight, seeing the continuous columns of Filipinos carrying stiff dead Filipinos in a shelter-half slung over a bamboo pole, carrying them over to throw them in the ditch because there were too many to bury, and then a column of Filipinos supporting other Filipinos, staggering to the hospital, and the hideous presence of death all about us."

V
Causes and Effects

18

The March of Death

In the United States, the fall of Bataan was a sad but not unexpected blow. For four months Americans had watched the gallant defense of the tiny peninsula with a mixture of pride and helplessness. Yet from the moment Japanese forces overran the rest of Luzon and swept on through the Philippines to the south, it had been clear that the fate of Bataan was sealed. On April 10, 1942, the headlines on their morning newspapers told readers in the United States that the inevitable had finally occurred.

The American defeat on Bataan came long after many other Allied outposts in the Pacific had fallen to the onrushing Japanese. So the nation's sorrow at its loss was tempered by admiration for the stubborn defense that had held out so long against a seemingly irresistible foe. Bataan would "take its place forever in the great traditions of the American people," commented the *New York Times*, reflecting, in these words, the reaction of many Americans.

A month later, the fall of Corregidor proved another hard blow for Americans to take, but soon the victories in the Coral Sea and at Midway and the successful landing on Guadalcanal reawakened the country's spirit and America's pride in her fighting forces. By the late summer of 1942, barely four months after General King's tragic surrender, it was clear that the Japanese had reached the limit of their means —and were being thrown back. The great counteroffensive that would drive them all the way back to Tokyo would soon begin.

The news of the fall of Bataan had not included word of the Death March, for there was no way in which the details of events following General King's surrender could have reached the outside world. The American people assumed that the men of the Luzon Force had been interned in prisoner of war camps, where they would remain until liberated by returning American armies. That the prisoners would be denied the consideration and decent treatment their gallant defense had earned them was a thought entertained by very few.

It was not until several months had passed, when stories of Japanese brutality began filtering back from the Pacific, that American authorities began to have grave fears for the safety of the troops captured on Bataan. In August, 1942, a group of Americans led by Ambassador Joseph C. Grew were repatriated from Japan on the liner *Gripsholm*. They told a shocking tale of harsh treatment at the hands of the Japanese. This report was followed by further accounts of Japanese atrocities sent back from Pacific battlefields and by the execution of three captured American aviators who had participated in the Doolittle raid on Tokyo.

Time after time the American State Department protested to the Japanese about such incidents. Time after time the United States requested that the International Red Cross be given access to prisoners in Japanese hands, that American food shipments be allowed to reach the prisoners, that full and accurate lists of names and locations of the captives be provided, that proper medicine and food be given the prisoners and that, in sum, the Japanese abide by the provisions of the Geneva Prisoner of War Convention.

While the Japanese answers to these protests were either unsatisfactory or nonexistent, it was not until mid-1943 that the American government really became aware of the extent of Japanese atrocities on Bataan. In April of that year three Americans, Captain William E. Dyess, Lieutenant Commander Melvin H. McCoy, and Major Stephen M. Mellnik, escaped from a prisoner of war camp in the southern Philippines. Assisted by Filipino guerrillas, they made their way to a rendezvous point and were picked up by an American submarine. In early July they reached General MacArthur's headquarters in Brisbane, Australia.

The story they had to tell of brutal mistreatment at the hands of the Japanese was the first authentic report that American authorities received of conditions in the Philippines. Only one of the three men, Captain Dyess, had participated in the Death March, but he provided a gruesome firsthand account of that event that shocked and upset his listeners.

Dyess, an Air Corps officer, had been taken prisoner on

April 9th, the day of the surrender. Assembled with a large group of Americans and Filipinos at the Mariveles airstrip the next morning, he was immediately a witness to some of the worst examples of Japanese brutality. And in the six days in which it took his group to reach O'Donnell, he and the others were subjected to further cruelty, indifference, and sadism. Men were beaten, robbed, killed, starved, denied water, and forbidden to assist each other. They were exposed to the most horrible tortures of the Death March.

All of this was clear in Dyess' mind. And as he recounted the savage details to the horrified American officers in Brisbane, they in turn were appalled and disgusted by the barbarity of the events he described.

General MacArthur wasted no time in forwarding to Washington the reports of the Death March by Dyess and of life in prison camp by McCoy and Mellnik, who had been captured on Corregidor. But it would be another six months before the American public would read them.

The delay in the release of the tragic story of the Death March was not a deliberate attempt to mislead the American people or to spare them the shock of the news. The main reason for this delay was the fear that publishing Dyess' frank report might expose the thousands of American prisoners in Japanese hands to further torture and punishment. United States authorities were also afraid that releasing the story might undermine efforts to persuade the Japanese to pass American shipments of food and medical supplies on to the captives.

Meanwhile, almost as soon as Dyess returned to the United States in the summer of 1943, newspaper and magazine editors got word of his shocking experiences. A chance item that had appeared earlier in the *New York Times* describing one of Dyess' exploits as a pilot in the Philippines had made a hero of him. The news of his escape, then, led reporters to ask for more details, and it was not long before they learned about the Death March. An association of about 100 newspapers, led by the *Chicago Tribune*, began a fight for permission to publish the story. By the beginning of 1944, journalistic pressure on the War Department had reached major proportions.

By now, also, it was clear to Washington that the official policy of silence had failed to alleviate in any way the lot of the prisoners. Releasing the details of Japanese atrocities could hardly make things any worse for the captives and, by exposing Japan to the light of world opinion, might even bring about some improvement in their condition. The shocking news of Bataan would also do much to combat any overoptimism or complacency that American victories in the Pacific were encouraging in the public mind.

On the morning of January 28, 1944, American newspapers carried screaming headlines announcing the Japanese cruelties on Bataan and in the Philippine prisoner of war camps. A joint War and Navy Department release, drawn from the reports of Dyess, McCoy, and Mellnik, and including long excerpts from them, was the basis of these headlines. News stories picked up the highlights of these reports and repeated them so as to emphasize their most shocking details. A few days later, the *Chicago Tribune* and other papers began running a serialized account by Dyess of his experiences. But the author, ironically, was dead, killed in an accident on

December 22nd while flying a new type of fighter plane that he had hoped to pilot in renewed combat against the Japanese.

The American reaction to the news of Bataan was one of shock, horror, sorrow, and deep anger. Especially stunned were the relatives of men captured on Bataan, who up to now had received no inkling of the fate of their loved ones. In towns like Maywood, Ill., Brainerd, Minn., or Salinas, Calif., which had given National Guard units to service in the Philippines, the entire community was affected. "Why haven't we been told this before?" one mother plaintively asked newspapermen. "We can take it, if only we are told about it. This is the most horrible thing I have heard of."

All over the country, indignant public officials, private citizens, social and fraternal groups, and newspaper and magazine editors called for revenge or, at the very least, a renewed effort to end the war in the Pacific and punish those Japanese responsible for the Bataan atrocities.

In the four Japanese relocation centers in California and Arizona, established to house Japanese and Japanese-Americans evacuated from the West Coast, guards were tightened and evacuees forbidden to leave their projects. Angry protests were raised in some nearby areas at the "soft" treatment accorded the evacuees. But inside the camp gates, meetings were being called to condemn the Death March. And the director of the Rivers, Ariz., center pointed out that more than two hundred Japanese-American relatives of the evacuees in his camp were serving in the Pacific. "If they fall into Japanese hands," he declared, "they will be treated worse than Americans."

The "March of Death," as it was immediately termed by the press, had made Americans angrier than at any time since Pearl Harbor. In Washington, Secretary of State Cordell Hull asserted that it would "be necessary to summon, to assemble together, all the demons available from anywhere and combine the fiendishness which all of them embody to describe the conduct of those who inflicted these unthinkable tortures on Americans and Filipinos." He promised that the victims of Bataan would some day be avenged. Evidence was being carefully gathered, Hull said, for the day when Allied victory would bring Japanese war criminals to the bar of justice.

Echoing the Secretary's words, former Ambassador Grew blamed the atrocities on the Japanese military caste and the ruthless system that it had developed. This ugly side of Japan, he grimly stated, must be completely crushed.

On Capitol Hill, the comments were even stronger. Representative Sol Bloom, chairman of the House Foreign Affairs Committee, warned the Japanese that they would have to pay for their actions. "We'll hold the rats—from the Emperor down to the lowest ditch digger—responsible for a million years if necessary." Senator Bennett Champ Clark called for bombing Japan "out of existence" and hanging the Emperor. "Gut the heart of Japan with fire," demanded Senator Lister Hill. The Japanese, said Senate Majority Leader Alben Barkley, should be "punished as though caught red-handed in murder upon the streets of our cities."

Senator Wallace H. White called for retribution to "be visited not alone on the Japanese Army, but on the authorities and people of Japan." While Senator Carl A. Hatch, referring to the Death March as a "throwback to barbarianism," proposed isolating the Japanese people on their home islands "forever."

Still another Senator, Richard B. Russell, declared that "the American Indian with his scalping knife and fiery stake was a chivalrous cavalier when compared to the Japanese." The United Nations, he insisted, must "keep faith with those who fell in the 'March of Death.' " And the Chairman of the House Military Affairs Committee, Andrew J. May, with perhaps less awareness of military capabilities than he should have had, demanded that the American fleet be sent at once to blow Tokyo off the map.

As one observer commented, if all the indignation in Washington could have been transformed into immediate military action, the war with Japan would have been ended in short order. And all over the country, a sudden rise in the sale of War Bonds indicated that the American people were doing their best to translate their anger into something more tangible. Sales in many parts of the nation doubled immediately. Almost everywhere they set new records. "Revenge! The Nation Demands It," read the headlines.

Even as the news of Bataan was being indignantly received in the United States, troops of the American 7th Division were pouring ashore on the beaches of Kwajalein in the central Pacific. Just before their landing, they had learned about the Death March. Their outrage, anger, and stated desire for revenge was no less violent than that of their civilian compatriots at home.

A war correspondent, anxious to see what would happen to a group of Japanese prisoners, followed them from their moment of capture to the time they left the island. He saw American soldiers sharing their food with the prisoners, corpsmen treating the wounded Japanese and gently placing them on stretchers, and sailors carefully raising the litters of the wounded to the decks of the transport that would carry them to a rear area hospital. The worst that befell the prisoners, reported the correspondent, "was a series of verbal reflections, delivered in a language they did not understand anyway, upon the legitimacy of their honorable ancestors."

19

The Alternatives

In the American mind, the Death March was a single, long column of walking prisoners, each constantly harried by brutal guards and subject to planned and well-organized atrocities in an over-all pattern of Japanese malice. This picture, inaccurate and misleading, was based almost entirely on Captain Dyess' shocking report, an account that was essentially the story of his own experiences.

Dyess had been in a group of men that had suffered the worst extremes of Japanese cruelty and indifference. That the experiences of other prisoners were not always identical with his was never made clear. That many were nowhere near as bad as his was equally unknown. Chance alone had dictated that he should escape to tell his story, just as chance had seen to it that his experiences were among the most horrifying of all and that they were taken by official Washington, the press, and the public as typical of what had happened to all of the prisoners.

It is hardly surprising, then, that most Americans viewed the Death March as the result of a deliberate Japanese policy to torture and kill the prisoners. How else explain the continuous mistreatment of men who had honorably surrendered? What other reason could lie behind the pattern of brutality and sadism described by Captain Dyess? Only a carefully planned and organized policy of deliberate cruelty could have brought about such an end.

Yet this was a view held more frequently by Americans who had never seen Bataan than by those who had been captured there. For the truth is that there was nothing deliberate or even well organized about the Death March. It was neither planned to happen as it did nor was it consciously and maliciously directed. It was, rather, the confused result of a tragic combination of circumstances, attitudes, and events.

The first and most obvious factor, a basic cause of the evils of the Death March, was the extremely poor physical condition of the prisoners. Fatigue, starvation, and disease had so reduced the strength of the Bataan defenders that the men who passed into Japanese hands on April 9th were barely shadows of their former selves. In the words of Colonel Harold W. Glattly, the former Luzon Force surgeon, they were "patients rather than prisoners."

Under normal circumstances, overlooking for the moment the physical mistreatment by the Japanese, the march to Camp O'Donnell would not have imposed an undue strain on healthy men. In general, the movement out of Bataan was a slow one. The average daily hike covered no more than ten or fifteen miles, hardly prohibitive for troops in good or even fair health.

The resources of the human body are amazing, enabling it to stand extreme trials and still continue to function. Thus the shortages of food and water would not have greatly affected a healthy prisoner. Nor would his needs have been so severe. No men would have dropped by the wayside because they were physically incapable of taking another step. The burning sun, the choking dust, the shocking trauma of defeat would all have been less punishing. Resting points along the route of march would have been crowded and far from comfortable, but they would not have been stained with the filth of diseased human waste and dead and dying bodies. That the sick men of the Luzon Force became even sicker as prisoners of war was due in large part to their condition at the time of the surrender, a condition that led inevitably to the spread of disease and the further weakening of the captured troops.

Had General King's troops been in good health—and the individual Japanese shown less brutality—the prisoners' march from Bataan would probably have differed little from other similar movements that took place during World War II. The American reader may recall the sight of long lines of captured Germans and Italians, pictured in his newspaper or magazine, walking back to Allied prisoner of war camps. In better health, and under different circumstances, the men of the Luzon Force might have appeared much the same. "The so-called Death March," wrote Colonel Glattly, "would have been nothing more than discomfort for those who were in good physical condition."

The fact that his prisoners were in so weak a state imposed

on General Homma the responsibility for taking extraordinary precautions to insure the health and safety of the captured men. Yet both Homma and his chief of staff, Major General Takaji Wachi, claim that Colonel Nakayama said nothing about the health of the Luzon Force troops when he reported the results of his meeting with General King. With no hint from Nakayama, recalled Homma, "I had no reason to make inquiry of the physical condition of the prisoners. I thought it was no worse than our own troops."

On this assumption, 14th Army staff officers were mainly concerned with the fact that they had captured roughly twice as many Filipinos and Americans as they had anticipated. And they did make some hasty revisions in their plan for handling the prisoners. Yet despite these changes, the plan for 40,000 captives expected to be in fair physical condition was not altered in any fundamental way. Basically, it remained in effect much as originally devised.

Just why Colonel Nakayama failed to report the condition of the Luzon Force troops is hard to understand, for General King took pains to explain the situation to the Japanese officer. Possibly the interpreter at the surrender did not explain this point correctly. Perhaps Nakayama did report it, but Generals Homma and Wachi found it more convenient to forget this report.

Whatever Nakayama told Homma, the 14th Army could probably have done little to improve the lot of the prisoners on such short notice. The Japanese themselves were low on food and eating short rations. Medical supplies and equipment were also limited. Their hospitals were overflowing and their medical staffs swamped with work.

Perhaps the captured men would have been able to recuperate if left in southern Bataan, but this was clearly impractical from the Japanese point of view. Not even General King expected the Luzon Force to remain on Bataan. Fifteen Japanese ambulances, half the entire number in the 14th Army, according to Homma's medical officer, were assigned the task of transporting sick or wounded prisoners. But this, of course, was far from enough.

But what of the other Japanese vehicles? Could these have been used to transport the captives? Japanese military units normally contained far fewer vehicles than did American units in World War II. The 14th Army did not have enough trucks and cars to satisfy its own requirements, and could not spare any to carry prisoners. Of the 300 to 400 trucks that General Homma had on April 9th, not more than 230 were in operating condition, and these were spread very thin. Quite a few, obviously, were needed to provide ammunition for the guns shelling Corregidor and to stockpile supplies in southern Bataan for the forthcoming amphibious assault on the island fortress. Still others were required to make daily runs from the shores of Lingayen Gulf in the north, where Japanese supplies were being landed, since the railroad from that area had been badly damaged during the fighting.

Gasoline was also limited. Japanese supply officers doled out the precious fuel with the motto, "a drop of gasoline is as precious as a drop of blood." So tight was the Japanese transportation situation that a large portion of the 14th Army then leaving Bataan on other missions was forced to move on foot. Troops of the 65th Brigade and 16th Division were marched out of Bataan in long columns and experienced many of the difficulties encountered by the American and Filipino prisoners. "An unsuitable selection of pace," complained one Japanese battalion commander, "caused the column to halt unnecessarily. . . . Malaria patients who had attacks of fever while on the march had a tendency to straggle, and were very difficult to deal with."

But if the Japanese were unable or unwilling to assume the burden of providing adequate transportation for their prisoners, they could have accepted General King's offer to use his own vehicles and gasoline to move the Luzon Force troops out of Bataan. To the American commander, it was obvious that his sick and hungry men would have a difficult time attempting to leave Bataan on foot, and he had told Colonel Nakayama that he had reserved sufficient fuel and transportation to carry his troops to a prison camp.

By using the already established administrative organization of the Luzon Force, King hoped that he could complete the evacuation of Bataan with a minimum of difficulty and hardship to all. Probably he planned to move the men by units, under their own officers, or through collecting points in the case of the totally disorganized II Corps, with medical aid stations set up along the way to help the weaker men. The Japanese would have had to provide food and additional medical supplies. Still, this or any other form of organized evacuation under American control would undoubtedly have worked better than the Japanese plan.

Yet, assuming the Japanese had agreed to follow King's recommendation, just how many Americans and Filipinos could actually have ridden out of Bataan? Despite King's statement to Nakayama, the supply of gasoline and the number of operational vehicles in the Luzon Force on April 9th was totally inadequate to move the entire command. At the time of the surrender, there were at most 1,200 vehicles, probably a great deal less, approximately 11,000 gallons of gas, and little or no grease or oil. And many of these vehicles, and a considerable amount of fuel, were destroyed by the troops themselves on the mistaken understanding that General King had ordered this to be done.

What General King had ordered destroyed was all military supplies *except* transportation. Vehicles, other than tanks, were to be left undamaged. But his orders were misunderstood, and large numbers of trucks, buses, sedans, and jeeps were put out of action. Some units simply destroyed all vehicles, others only "military" vehicles, interpreting this to mean anything other than civilian buses or cars. In one motor pool, the men drained all the oil from the trucks and sedans and then started the engines racing as fast as they could. A tank battalion fired armor-piercing shells into its truck motors, then dumped gasoline into the cabs and bodies and set them afire. Another unit poured sand into the gas tanks and crankcases of its jeeps.

Given this wholesale destruction of vehicles, the distance to be traveled out of Bataan, even to San Fernando, the capacity and very poor condition of the remaining vehicles, and the state of the Bataan roads, it seems doubtful that as many as half the men in the Luzon Force could have been spared from having to walk. Yet even this number was probably more than were permitted to ride by the Japanese. And if American officers had been directing the evacuation, seats in vehicles would have gone to the sickest and weakest men, those who eventually were the first to drop by the wayside when they made the march from Bataan.

Since the 14th Army was no better—and probably worse —equipped than the Luzon Force to move the prisoners from Bataan, the Japanese refusal of General King's request sealed the fate of many of the captives.

There are several possible reasons for this refusal. For the defenders of Bataan, the war was over, but for Homma much remained to be done. Corregidor still prevented Japanese use of Manila Bay, and in the mountains of northern Luzon and on many of the other islands of the Philippine archipelago thousands of Filipinos and Americans were still holding out, or were not yet even under attack. In Tokyo, Homma's superiors were demanding that the Philippine campaign, already behind schedule, be brought to a rapid conclusion. Indeed, staff officers from Imperial General Headquarters were already on Luzon to observe operations and encourage their acceleration.

In order to attack Corregidor as soon as possible, Homma was anxious to clear southern Bataan of his prisoners as quickly as he could. He was also faced with the problem of rapidly moving supplies and equipment forward to support his assault on the island fortress.

Perhaps the 14th Army staff officers reasoned that they themselves could move the prisoners better and faster than could General King. Even if they couldn't, to allow King to do it would have been an open admission of this, and involve a serious loss of face before both the enemy and their superiors. Possibly they felt they needed the American vehicles to supplement their own meager transportation, that this was more important than moving the prisoners. Or they may have regarded King's proposal as a ruse, a delaying maneuver to slow down preparations for the Corregidor attack. Perhaps, finally, they were so indifferent to the fate of the prisoners that they did not stop to consider which was the best or most efficient way to move the captured men. They chose what probably appeared at first glance to be the easiest method of clearing southern Bataan.

From almost any point of view, the Japanese choice was a bad one. The 14th Army did indeed use captured Luzon Force vehicles to supplement Japanese trucks and ambulances in transporting a good many of the prisoners, but General King could probably have moved as many or more. An American-run operation would have moved the weakest men. The Japanese do not appear to have let a man's physical condition affect his status as either a pedestrian or a rider. Had the Luzon Force staff conducted the evacuation, it would have been more orderly. Certainly there would have been no atrocities. And southern Bataan might have been emptied of Luzon Force troops in a shorter period of time.

20

A Failure of Leadership

The tragic evacuation of the prisoners from Bataan was marked by confusion, inconsistency, and disorganization. There was almost a complete lack of pattern in the way the movement was conducted. Indeed, if there were any plan to mistreat or kill the prisoners, as has sometimes been charged, it was certainly administered in a haphazard and uncoordinated fashion. The lot of a prisoner of war is seldom a happy one, yet many of the captives were relatively well treated. They rode in vehicles or walked at a slow pace, sometimes without guards, were able to eat or drink, and were not molested. Others were beaten, starved, refused water, hurried along by brutal sentries, or otherwise mistreated. Many were killed. No two groups of men had the same specific experience.

The inconsistencies in the Japanese attitude and behavior are best exemplified in the varied actions of the guards. Most of these were transportation troops under General Kawane, Homma's chief of transportation, but many combat troops were also assigned as guards initially or for brief periods along the route of march. There seems to have been no difference in the behavior of the Japanese combat and service troops. Combat troops—probably soldiers of the 65th Brigade —carried out the massacre of Filipino officers and noncoms of the 91st Division. But other, or perhaps even the same, troops of the 65th Brigade moved prisoners along the road above Balanga apparently without incident. Similar discrepancies can be found in the actions of Japanese transportation troops. Even the treatment of the captured men by Japanese medical officers differed, as events at the two Luzon Force general hospitals bear witness.

Colonel Nakayama asserted that the Japanese were "not barbarians," and General Homma and others spoke warmly to Americans of how well they would be treated. But the actions of many Japanese officers and men often belied these statements.

That the movement from Bataan lacked any definite pattern shows only too well how quickly the evacuation disintegrated into complete disorder. The 14th Army plan, inadequate to begin with, was not sufficiently modified or corrected to fit the circumstances with which the Japanese suddenly found themselves confronted. More important was the fact that the Japanese execution of the plan was so inept. The guidance and leadership that might have been expected from Japanese officers, and which should have prevented many of the atrocities, was completely lacking.

General Wachi, the 14th Army chief of staff, said after the

war that he understood there was a strong feeling among some of Homma's superiors that the Filipino prisoners should be "severely dealt with." Indeed, according to Wachi, one inspecting officer from Tokyo argued that if the Filipino soldiers were not sufficiently cowed by harsh treatment before their release they would become the centers of anti-Japanese activities in their home villages. But these sentiments do not appear to have carried much weight with Homma. Certainly there is no evidence that they were ever officially applied.

Many Americans who were captured on Bataan felt that the brutal treatment they received was a deliberate attempt to humiliate them in front of the Filipinos, to demonstrate the humbling of the white man in a new "Asia for the Asiatics." But if this were so, why then were the Filipinos so cruelly mistreated? Furthermore, most of the higher-ranking Americans were treated relatively well. Had the Japanese really wanted to humiliate their American captives, it would have been far more effective to have devised some extremely debasing treatment for General King and his highest officers and to have administered it with great fanfare and publicity, while at the same time extending to the Filipinos the warm hand of friendship and cooperation. Since no such course was followed, this theory can probably be discarded.

But if there was no deliberate attempt by the Japanese to punish the Americans and Filipinos, no one appears to have been overly concerned about the plight of the prisoners. At 14th Army headquarters, General Homma and his staff had their hands full with preparations for future operations, and either did not have the time to look more closely into the evacuation of the captives, or did not care to.

Satisfied that the original plan for the prisoners was as good as could be devised under the circumstances, the 14th Army commander felt confident that he could leave its execution to his subordinates. "It was not my place to interfere with them," he explained after the war. "I trusted that everything they could do under the circumstances they [would] do to their utmost ability."

From his forward command post near Lamao and his Balanga headquarters, Homma himself would occasionally see the prisoners move by when he took time out from his work. He claimed that nothing he saw or that was reported to him indicated "anything extraordinary." Not until three and one-half years later did he learn from American newspapermen that the movement of the prisoners from Bataan had been given the name of the "Death March." And not until he was on trial for his life in a Manila courtroom for what had happened on Bataan did he learn "for the first time," said Homma, "of such atrocities." If "these atrocities" actually occurred, he continued, "I am ashamed of myself."

Before the war Homma had come under considerable criticism in the Japanese Army because he was regarded as being pro-British and, by extension, pro-American. A military student in pre-World War I England and an observer with the British Expeditionary Force in France, Homma had also served in India and as military attaché in London. He had received a British military decoration and spoke English well. He was regarded by his subordinates as just and humane, and as a strict disciplinarian when it came to dealing with Japanese troops who got out of hand in occupied areas. Once the Philippine campaign was ended, he seems to have had a liberal attitude toward the Filipino citizens, hoping to win them over by kindness. Indeed, in May, 1942, Field Marshal Count Hisaichi Terauchi, commander of all Japanese forces in the "southern area," is reported to have rebuked Homma for being "too soft" in his treatment of the Filipinos.

Yet, despite all this, Homma seems to have paid little attention to the brutality of his men on Bataan. The record of 14th Army court-martial cases during the period of Homma's command in the Philippines supports his reputation for punishing Japanese soldiers who mistreated civilians. But this record reveals not a single instance of a soldier being tried for cruelty to a prisoner of war. Homma's protests that he knew nothing of the Death March may well have been true. Whether or not he should have known about it is of course another matter.

During his postwar trial, Homma accepted the blame for the acts of his subordinates by agreeing that he was "morally responsible for everything that happened." But this moral responsibility, he argued, was purely "technical." "I could not think," he wrote to his defense counsel after the trial, "that the commander in chief could be punished by death for his moral responsibility." Unfortunately for Homma, his judges thought otherwise.

The 14th Army transportation officer, General Kawane, who was responsible for moving the prisoners from Balanga to O'Donnell, was also apparently too busy to give the Luzon Force move the attention it needed. In addition to evacuating the captured troops and rushing preparations to receive them at Camp O'Donnell, Kawane was charged with the important and probably overriding mission of transporting supplies and equipment to southern Bataan for the Corregidor assault. With all units of the 14th Army assigned to other missions, there were very few infantry troops available to assist him. His transportation troops and staff were spread thin, and he himself had little rest. It seems evident that the bulk of his energies were not directed toward close supervision of the movement of the prisoners.

A lack of concern about the captives is even more apparent among lower ranking officers of the 14th Army. Many of them not only witnessed the Death March but were themselves also guilty of many of the crimes committed against the prisoners. Except in a few instances, they exercised little or no control over their troops and displayed an appalling indifference and callousness to the suffering of the captives.

Given the failure or indifference of Japanese leadership, the fact that General Homma and his staff did not plan or intend the harsh treatment accorded the prisoners is almost irrelevant. The Japanese soldier of World War II was inclined neither by custom nor training to act kindly toward a captured foe. That his officers, well aware of this attitude, provided no effective guidance shows a glaring weakness in the structure of the 14th Army if not, indeed, in the entire Japanese military organization.

The brutality and callousness displayed by the Japanese soldier on Bataan is difficult to understand when measured against Western standards of mercy and compassion. Yet cruelty and indifference to suffering were strongly rooted in the Japanese character. They were the results of hundreds of years of violence, treachery, and suspicion, of a difficult, competitive existence in a crowded land where human life was the cheapest of commodities, and of a deliberate indoctrination. An understanding of these factors helps to explain, while it cannot condone, the tragic events of the Death March.

The Japanese Army was a true reflection of the authoritarian and compulsive society from which it sprang. Military life was a harsh existence where discipline was brutally enforced and human suffering callously ignored. From the day he entered the Army, the Japanese soldier was indoctrinated into a system that demanded swift, unquestioning obedience and rewarded dissenters or laggards with sure and immediate punishment. While long since abolished in Western armies, and even forbidden officially in the Japanese military service, physical chastisement was frequent and severe. The soldier was quick to obey an order from a superior, even if the two men were only a rank apart, if he was not to receive a blow or a kick for his tardiness. Any slight hint of a challenge to authority was severely punished.

Life in the Army was never easy, but the first three months were the hardest. Recruits who failed to show proper respect and deference or to wash the clothes or clean the boots of older or higher ranking soldiers were frequently beaten into insensibility. Their superiors struck them with the open hand or clenched fist, kicked them with their nailed boots, or beat them mercilessly with rifles, swords, or bayonet sheaths. These acts reflected and magnified customs of Japanese civil life, where policemen struck citizens, teachers hit students, and corporal punishment was a common occurrence within families.

The Japanese officer or noncom administered physical punishment ostensibly to enforce discipline, but a sudden whim or bad mood might easily cause him to strike a subordinate without reason. There was a standard army joke that the officer hit the sergeant, the sergeant hit the corporal, the corporal hit the superior private, the superior private hit the private first class, the private first class hit the private second class, and the private second class, with no one below him to hit, went down to the stable and kicked a horse.

While the Japanese soldier might joke about his lot, he could not question it. If disciplined, he had no recourse to higher authority, for to doubt the right of a superior to do anything at all was in itself a breach of military discipline. The soldier had to stand at attention while he was being beaten or kicked by his superior. If he fell, he had to get up, resume the position of attention, and submit to more punishment.

On one occasion, witnessed by American prisoners, a Japanese sergeant was putting some recruits through bayonet practice. One of the men was a little slow or awkward in his movements. The sergeant suddenly halted the drill and called the offender to attention. Then, as the recruit stiffened, erect, the sergeant struck him blow after blow in the face with his fist. Each time the sergeant hit him, the man staggered, but each time he resumed his stance of attention. Finally, the sergeant put all his weight behind a tremendous kick. Then, as if nothing had happened, the drill was resumed. "I have personally seen these Japanese beaten unconscious," recalled one American who had been taken prisoner. "They had to be carried to their quarters."

Many recruits committed suicide during their training period because they could not stand the brutal treatment meted out to them.

Accustomed to administering or enduring harsh physical punishment, the Japanese soldier was prone to ignore the sufferings of even his own comrades. On April 10th on Bataan, American prisoners watching a column of Japanese troops march by saw one of the soldiers stumble and fall to the ground. The Japanese was apparently completely worn out, for he lay motionless, unable to rise. A noncom walked over to the man, ordered him up sharply and, when this had no effect, struck him several heavy blows in the face. The soldier still remained on the ground, so the noncom began to kick him. None of the other Japanese paid any attention to this incident until finally, at the direction of the noncom, two privates picked the man up and pushed him into the column. Somehow he managed to stagger forward, to the shocked amazement of the watching Americans.

Elsewhere a Japanese enlisted man, stricken with malaria, was running a high fever. But his superior, he noted in his diary, "never believed me and he was so sarcastic about my sickness." "I did not know," he wrote the next day, "that my comrades were so cruel to a sick man. Every one of them has been so sarcastic they even insulted me. I would like to die. . . ."

The Japanese soldier was thus the product of a stern and unfeeling military system that produced a blind obedience on the one hand and a brutal indifference on the other. He endured punishment stoically, but administered it with an emotional, often sadistic unreasonableness and inconsistency. The harsh treatment of the American and Filipino prisoners on Bataan reflected in great part the brutality to which their captors were themselves normally subjected. Shocking as it was to those unfamiliar with life in Japan, it did not represent a cruelty abnormal for the average Japanese.

The Japanese code of *Bushido*—the "way of the warrior" of which many Americans had heard so much—offered a prisoner no protection against brutality. Westerners tended to think of *Bushido* as analogous to "chivalry," knighthood's strict code of honor that emphasized the duty of the strong to assist and protect the weak. But *Bushido*, while just as severe in its dictates, put its stress on loyalty and self-sacrifice. It had no tradition of mercy or compassion, and sanctioned, if it did not actually encourage, deceit and cruelty in the performance of duty to a superior. Unlike a Western knight, the traditional Japanese warrior did not ride forth to rescue damsels, which he would have considered a preposterous notion, or to uplift the downtrodden, the thought of which would have equally amused him. And neither he nor his modern descendant felt obligated to extend a compassionate hand to a fallen foe.

The very fact that the men of the Luzon Force had allowed themselves to be taken prisoner increased the severity of their treatment. For the Japanese, to become a prisoner was the ultimate disgrace. Death in action, or if necessary by suicide, was preferred to surrender. "Do not fall captive even if the alternative is death," Japanese troops were told. "Bear in mind the fact that to be captured not only means disgracing the Army, but your parents and family will never be able to hold their heads up again. Always save the last round for yourself."

The tradition of suicide rather than surrender, long ingrained in the warrior class in Japan, was passed on to the World War II conscript army and accepted blindly by the unquestioning soldier. Indeed, to be taken captive "while still able to resist" was a criminal act, punishable in extreme cases by death. The disgrace of becoming a prisoner was so great that Japanese troops considered it a duty to kill their own wounded rather than to permit them to be captured. Japanese soldiers taken prisoner during the war were terrified that their status might become known to their families and friends at home. Most of them expected death or severe punishment on their return to Japan.

That the American prisoners on Bataan were not ashamed of having surrendered was difficult for their captors to understand. And the Japanese were all the more shocked that the prisoners should want to have their names reported to the American government so their relatives would know they were still alive.

Two Japanese sergeants told Colonel Ernest B. Miller that the Luzon Force should never have surrendered, even when the battle was obviously over. They agreed that further resistance would have gained nothing, but pointed out that the Japanese would have been greatly impressed if all of the Filipinos and Americans had died fighting. Another Japanese offered his pistol to Major Eugene C. Jacobs and courteously asked if Jacobs would like to kill himself. When Jacobs declined, his captor was surprised.

The Japanese soldier, in General Homma's words, "despised beyond description" his fellow countrymen who allowed themselves to be captured. Since this was so, the Japanese looked upon an enemy who had surrendered with even stronger contempt. The brutality with which a Japanese soldier treated his subordinate in the normal course of events would hardly seem excessive to him when dealing with a disgraced enemy prisoner for whom he had little love in the first place.

The first few hours of his captivity are normally the most dangerous ones for a prisoner of war. For few soldiers who have seen their friends die and have themselves experienced the blood and grime of battle feel much initial sympathy for an enemy prisoner who may have contributed to their suffering. This was true of the Japanese soldier as well as any other. Indeed, the heat and passions of war, the vengeful feelings and vindictiveness which spring from physical combat were all too readily reflected in the highly emotional Japanese soldier. They helped to reawaken the warrior tradition of revenge, long rooted in the Japanese national character and strengthened and secured in the soldier by persistent indoctrination.

For the Japanese, the act of revenge was just and honorable, with a clear, traditional sanction. A function of loyalty and duty, it was strongly linked with the code of *Bushido*. In the history of Japan, men had become national heroes for acts of vengeance, even though in committing them they had completely ignored what the Western mind regarded as basic ethical behavior.

Japanese documents captured during World War II contain frequent references to revenge. The diary of a 14th Army soldier wounded on Bataan is a good example:

In San Fernando there was one carload of prisoners. . . . Thinking that we got injured by these natives, I could not help get mad.

The soldiers were all saying "Kill every last one of them" and "don't let them eat." At any rate the greater percentage of my comrades were injured by them. Seventy to eighty percent of us were killed by these natives! Who wouldn't get mad.

Individual acts of brutality were thus often motivated by the desire to avenge a fallen comrade. The slaughter of the officers and noncoms of the 91st Philippine Army Division, for example, may well have been the product of just such feelings.

The great differences between the Americans and Japanese in language, customs, training, and discipline also contributed to the horrors of the Death March. Such differences were particularly hard to adjust since the Japanese usually demanded that any adjustments be made by their prisoners. The Japanese soldier, unquestioningly carrying out orders from above, could not stop to reason with a prisoner who seemed to be disobeying him. Nor, in most cases, was he personally so inclined. The prisoners themselves, sick, exhausted and ordered about in a strange tongue, often found themselves completely confused by their brusque and impatient captors. The lack of coordination and order puzzled them even more. They were increasingly bewildered by the strange actions of the Japanese.

"You didn't know what they wanted," recalled Captain

Alberto Abeleda. "Sometimes they tell you this, and if you don't understand they beat you right away. . . . At first they told us that we were all free; that we can go home now. . . . Then . . . we were being guarded. So I really cannot tell you what they wanted, for I really don't know."

When a Japanese soldier gave an order, he did not customarily see fit to explain it in any more detail than he felt was absolutely necessary for its execution. Thus, when two or three guards were given the job of taking a group of 100 prisoners up the road, they probably were told little more than their immediate destination. How far the prisoners had already come, when they had last rested or tasted food and water, and how much farther they had to go beyond the next stopping point was information that a guard would neither expect nor receive. Certainly he would not dare to request it. All the Japanese soldier knew was that he was responsible for moving a large number of prisoners a certain distance, probably within a given time, and that he would be severely punished if any captive escaped.

When prisoners dropped out from exhaustion, or sought water beside the road, the Japanese guard was faced with a dilemma. If he thought the men were attempting to escape, it was easily and quickly solved. And, of course, if a guard actually believed prisoners were trying to get away, even the Geneva Convention did not forbid him to stop them. But if a prisoner simply fell down in the middle of the road, a difficult problem was created. The Japanese could not leave the long column of marching men he had been directed to guard in order to remain with those who fell behind. If he did, the men still in the column might escape. Nor, on the other hand, could he leave anyone behind who might later recover and get away.

The Japanese soldier was not accustomed to thinking for himself. He was usually told what to do and how to do it, and individual initiative was discouraged. Left to himself and faced with a seemingly insoluble dilemma, his normal tendency was to become excited, even hysterical. Hence the frenzied blows and kicks rained on the fallen prisoners and the ultimate bayonet thrust or rifle shot which solved the guard's problem and put everything neatly back in its place.

The harsh discipline and unquestioning obedience to orders with which the Japanese soldier was inculcated had other effects, of which the crowded assembly areas, the packed warehouse at Lubao, and the jammed boxcars are ready examples. The guards were probably told to place their charges in a given area or building. It mattered not that there were soon too many prisoners for the space provided. Japanese soldiers carried out their orders exactly as they received them. To have questioned the wisdom of these orders, or to have admitted their own inability to follow them, would have been unnatural.

The brutality of the Japanese soldier's training and the rough discipline of his army did not in any way excuse the harsh treatment of the prisoners. Such treatment, like physical punishment within the Japanese Army, was specifically forbidden in Japanese prisoner of war regulations. The Emperor himself had commanded his troops to treat prisoners of war as "unfortunate individuals" and with "the utmost benevolence and kindness." The Japanese *Senjin-kun* ("Code of the Battlefield") had several passages forbidding the mistreatment of prisoners. And, most specifically, there was a standard *Rikutatsu* ("Army Instruction"), in force since 1904, outlining detailed rules for the handling of prisoners of war. These contained the clear injunction that "prisoners of war shall be treated with a spirit of goodwill and shall never be subjected to cruelties or humiliation." *

If the Japanese soldier was so well disciplined that he obeyed orders instantly and without question, it should follow that he would also obey standard army regulations. That he ignored them, for his fellow countrymen as well as for prisoners of war, clearly shows a failure on the part of his officers to provide proper leadership and guidance. On Bataan the results were fatal.

* * *

For the Americans and Filipinos of the Luzon Force who suffered through the difficult fighting on Bataan, April was indeed "the cruelest month." Sick, starving, exhausted, they entered the vale of captivity and met a horror they never foresaw.

The agony they endured, the death they often welcomed were not deviously and maliciously planned. Instead they were the result of four tragic conditions.

The first was the incredibly low physical state to which the Bataan defenders had sunk by April 9, 1942.

The second was the Japanese unpreparedness to receive so many prisoners in such a weakened condition, their inability to do much to improve this condition, and their unwillingness to accept General King's solution.

---

* This "Army Instruction" is reproduced as Appendix A.

The third was the cruelty and callousness of the individual Japanese soldier, whose training, instinct, and experience stifled the Western virtues of mercy and understanding.

The fourth, and perhaps the most important, was the failure of Japanese leadership.

Taken alone, any of these conditions might have been overcome. Together they produced the brutal, disorganized movement that has come to be known as the Death March.

Appendices

Appendix A

JAPANESE ARMY REGULATIONS
FOR HANDLING PRISONERS OF WAR

These regulations were issued in February, 1904, as Army Instruction No. 22 of that year, and subsequently revised on several occasions. They were the official regulations in force for all units and members of the Japanese Army in World War II.

Regulations for the handling of prisoners of war shall be as follows:

CHAPTER I
General Rules

Article 1. The term prisoner(s) of war as used in these regulations shall refer to combatants of enemy nationality or to those who by treaty or custom are entitled to treatment as prisoners of war.

Article 2. Prisoners of war shall be treated with a spirit of goodwill and shall never be subjected to cruelties or humiliation.

Article 3. Prisoners of war shall be given suitable treatment in accordance with their position and rank. However, those who fail to reply with sincerity and truth to questions regarding name and rank, and violators of other rules, shall not be included in this.

Article 4. Prisoners of war shall be required to conform to the discipline and regulations of the Imperial Army. Beyond this, their persons shall not be subjected to unwarranted restriction.

Article 5. Insofar as military discipline and moral standards are not affected, prisoners of war shall have freedom of religion and shall be permitted to attend worship in accordance with their respective sects.

Article 6. In case of disobedience it shall be permissible to hold a prisoner of war in confinement or detention or to subject him to other necessary disciplinary action. In case a prisoner of war attempts to escape, he may be stopped by armed force and if necessary killed or wounded.

Article 7. When a prisoner of war not under oath is captured in attempted escape, he shall be subjected to disciplinary action.

When such a prisoner of war, after successful escape, is again made prisoner of war, no punishment shall be inflicted for the previous escape.

Article 8. The methods of disciplining prisoners of war shall, besides following the foregoing articles, be in accordance with the provisions of the army regulation for minor punishments. Criminal acts of prisoners of war shall be tried by army court-martial.

CHAPTER II
Capture and Transportation to the Rear
Of Prisoners of War

Article 9. When a person to be treated as a prisoner of war is captured, his personal belongings shall be immediately inspected, and weapons, ammunition and other articles which may be put to military use shall be confiscated. Other belongings shall either be held in deposit or shall be left in his possession as circumstances require.

Article 10. When, among the prisoners of war mentioned in the foregoing article, there are officers who should be treated with special honor, an army commander or independent divisional commander may permit them to carry their own swords.

In such cases the names of the prisoners of war together with the reasons shall be reported to Imperial General Headquarters, from whence due notice shall be transmitted to the Ministry of War. The weapons which had been carried shall be held in deposit in the prisoners of war camp.

Article 11. Commanders of armies and of independent divisions shall, upon negotiations with the enemy forces after combat, be permitted to return or exchange captured sick and wounded prisoners of war who swear on oath not to take part in combat during the remainder of the same war.

In such case, names, total number and reasons shall be reported to Imperial General Headquarters from whence the Ministry of War shall be duly notified.

Article 12. Each unit capturing prisoners shall duly interrogate said prisoners, prepare a roster containing the name, age, rank, home address, home unit and place and date of wounding; a prisoner of war diary; and inventories of articles confiscated or held in deposit in accordance with the provisions of Article 9.

When, as provided for in the next foregoing article, the return, exchange or release on oath of prisoners of war are effected, the fact shall be noted on the prisoner of war roster.

Article 13. Prisoners of war shall be divided into officers and warrant officers and under and shall be transported under guard to the nearest line of communications command or transport and communications organization.

When this is done, the articles held in deposit, prisoner of war rosters, prisoner of war diaries and inventories shall be forwarded together with the captured personnel.

Article 14. Army units, line of communications commands or transport and communications organizations may, upon conference on the handing over of PW's by a naval commanding officer, receive into custody those prisoners of war together with deposited articles, rosters, diaries, and inventories.

Article 15. Commanders of armies or independent divisions shall promptly report to Imperial General Headquarters the number of prisoners of war they desire to send to the rear. Imperial General Headquarters shall inform the Ministry of War thereof.

Article 16. When the Ministry of War is in receipt of the information mentioned in the foregoing Article 15, it shall report to the Imperial General Headquarters the post or other location where the reception of prisoners of war will be effected. Imperial General Headquarters shall inform the Ministry of War regarding the expected date of arrival at the designated point.

The same procedure shall be followed when the Ministry of War has been informed regarding the reception of prisoners taken by the Navy.

Article 17. Line of communications commands and transport and communications organizations which in accordance with Articles 13 and 14 have accepted prisoners of war shall transport said prisoners of war under guard to the location(s) mentioned in the next foregoing article and shall there transfer said PW's together with deposited articles, PW rosters, PW diaries and inventories to the custody of the officer of the War Ministry charged with reception.

Article 18. When no Imperial General Headquarters is established, "Imperial General Headquarters" in this chapter shall be taken to read "General Staff Headquarters."

CHAPTER III

Accommodation and Control
Of Prisoners of War

Article 19. (Rescinded)

Article 20. For prisoners of war accommodations, army establishments, temples or other buildings which suffice to prevent escape and are not detrimental to the health and honor of the prisoners shall be utilized.

Article 21. The army commander or garrison area commander under whose jurisdiction comes the administration of Prisoner of War camps (hereinafter to be referred to as the High Administrator of PW camps) shall determine "regulations concerning PW camp duties" and shall make a report thereof to the Minister of War and duly inform the Director General of the PW Information Bureau.

Article 22. (Rescinded)

Article 23. (Rescinded)

Article 24. (Rescinded)

Article 25. (Rescinded)

Article 26. Insofar as mail sent and received by prisoners of war is, by international treaty, exempted from postage dues, the High Administrator of PW camps shall confer with the Post Office in the vicinity of the PW accommodations and shall determine a suitable procedure for the handling of postal matters.

Article 27. Rules and regulations concerning control within PW camps shall be determined by the High Administrator.

CHAPTER IV
Miscellaneous Rules

Article 28. Those enemy sick and wounded who, after medical treatment at dressing stations or hospitals, are considered incapable of military service shall, after due promise not to serve in the same war, be returned to their homes. However, those who have important relations with the conduct of the war are not included in this.

Article 29. Articles belonging to the prisoners of war and held in deposit by Imperial Government offices shall be restored to their possession at the time of their release.

Article 30. In case of the death of a prisoner of war, the money and possessions of the deceased shall be sent to the Prisoner of War Information Bureau by the unit, organization, hospital or dressing station concerned. When the belongings are of a perishable nature, such shall be sold and the proceeds of the sale shall be forwarded instead.

Article 31. The last will and testament of a deceased prisoner of war shall be handled in the same way as that of Japanese military personnel by the unit, organization, hospital or dressing station concerned, and shall be duly forwarded to the Prisoner of War Information Bureau.

Article 32. (Rescinded)

Article 33. Direct welfare activities for the benefit of prisoners of war by organizations legally established for charitable purposes may be permitted on submittal of a written pledge to the effect that no infractions or violations of the rules and regulations concerning prisoners will be made.

Appendix B

SENIOR COMMAND AND STAFF ON BATAAN

AMERICAN

Luzon Force: Major General Edward P. King, Jr.
  Chief of Staff: Brigadier General Arnold J. Funk
  G-1 (Personnel): Colonel Floyd Marshall
  G-2 (Intelligence): Lieutenant Colonel Frank L. Holland
  G-3 (Operations): Colonel James V. Collier
  G-4 (Supply): Colonel Roy C. Hilton
  Quartermaster: Colonel Charles S. Lawrence
  Transportation: Colonel Michael Quinn
  Surgeon: Lieutenant Colonel Harold W. Glattly
I Corps: Major General Albert M. Jones
II Corps: Major General George M. Parker, Jr.

JAPANESE

14th Army: Lieutenant General Masaharu Homma
  Chief of Staff: Major General Takaji Wachi
  1st Section (Operations): Colonel Motoo Nakayama
    Operations: Colonel Yoshio Nakajima
    Intelligence: Lieutenant Colonel Hikaru Haba
  2nd Section (Administration and Logistics): Colonel Toshimitsu Takatsu
    Supply: Major Moriya Wada
    Transportation: Major General Yoshikata Kawane

Medical: Colonel Shusuke Horiguchi
4th Division: Lieutenant General Kenzo Kitano
16th Division: Lieutenant General Susumu Morioka
21st Brigade: Major General Kameichiro Nagano
65th Brigade: Lieutenant General Akira Nara

A Note on Sources

This book is the product of many men's experiences. As such, it is based primarily on the testimony of hundreds of individuals who took part in, witnessed, or were in some way responsible for the events of April, 1942, that have come to be known as the Bataan Death March. Thus, while I have consulted many published sources, the best and most valuable information has come from unpublished and sometimes even unwritten accounts.

The most important single collection of material is the transcript and exhibits of the war crimes trial of General Homma, held in Manila in early 1946: "United States of America vs. Masaharu Homma, before the Military Commission convened by the Commanding General, United States Army Forces Western Pacific," a copy of which is on file in the World War II Records Division, National Archives, Alexandria, Va. The record of the trial includes important statements by Americans and Filipinos who participated in or witnessed the Death March, as well as equally valuable testimony by many Japanese who were connected with this event in one way or another. A massive collection of thirty volumes of testimony and an additional 400 or more separate statements, it is invaluable for any study of the Death March.

On the American and Filipino side, I have drawn important material from personal interviews and correspondence with survivors of Bataan. Much of this serves to modify or put in a clearer context some of the testimony at General Homma's trial, where the extreme aspects of the Death March were emphasized and where a balanced picture did not always emerge.

Of the many participants in the Death March whose testimony has proved valuable, I should like in particular to thank the following: Major General Albert M. Jones, Brigadier General James O. Gillespie, and Colonels Irvin E. Alexander, Donald D. Blackburn, James V. Collier, Virgil N. Cordero, Allan M. Cory, Malcolm V. Fortier, Charles A. Francis, Harold W. Glattly, Eugene C. Jacobs, Paul H. Krauss, Ray M. O'Day, Alexander S. Quintard, Jack W. Schwartz, John K. Wallace, and Frederick J. Yeager. These men served in a variety of ranks and capacities all over Bataan, and their experiences helped me to reconstruct a broad picture of events. Statements or narratives by more than a score of other participants or witnesses, on file in the Office of the Chief of Military History, Department of the Army, Washington, D.C., were also valuable.

The official report of the American Army in the Philippines, including accounts by General King and other commanders and staff on Bataan and Corregidor, was a useful source of material on the campaign itself and on some of the events that followed. Entitled "Report of USAFFE and USFIP in the Philippine Islands, 1941–1942," it was submitted by General Wainwright to the War Department in 1946. Copies are located in the Office of Military History and in the World War II Records Division of the National Archives.

Among published materials, the most important single volume is the official U.S. Army history of the Philippine campaign, Louis Morton, *The Fall of the Philippines* (Washington: Government Printing Office, 1953), a solid work on which I have drawn heavily for details of the fight for Bataan.

Several accounts by veterans of Bataan have also proved valuable: Major Bert Bank, *Back from the Living Dead* (Tuscaloosa, Ala.: privately printed, 1945); Lieutenant Colonel William E. Chandler, "The 26th Cavalry (PS) Battles to Glory," *Armored Cavalry Journal*, March–August, 1947; Major Calvin Ellsworth Chunn (ed.), *Of Rice and Men* (Los Angeles: Veterans' Publishing Company, 1946); Colonel V. N. Cordero, *My Experiences During the War With Japan* (Nuremberg, Germany: privately printed, no date); Lieutenant Colonel William E. Dyess, *The*

Dyess Story (New York: G. P. Putnam's Sons, 1944); Robert W. Levering, *Horror Trek* (Dayton, Ohio: The Horstman Printing Company, 1948); Colonel E. B. Miller, *Bataan Uncensored* (Long Prairie, Minn.: The Hart Publications, Inc., 1949); Reynaldo Perez, "Escape," in Manuel E. Buenafe (ed.), *The Voice of the Veteran, Memorial Edition* (Manila, P.I.: Republic Promotion, 1946); Colonel R. W. Volckmann, *We Remained* (New York: W. W. Norton & Company, Inc., 1954); General Jonathan M. Wainwright, *General Wainwright's Story* (Garden City, N.Y.: Doubleday and Company, Inc., 1946); and Alfred M. Weinstein, *Barbed-Wire Surgeon* (New York: The Macmillan Company, 1948).

Lieutenant Henry G. Lee, *Nothing But Praise* (Culver City, Calif.: Murray and Gee, Inc., 1948) is a book of poetry by a survivor of the Death March. The lines quoted from this slim volume are used through the courtesy of Lieutenant Lee's mother, Mrs. Mabel G. Marble.

Some pertinent material also appears in Colonel William C. Braly, *The Hard Way Home* (Washington: Infantry Journal Press, 1947); Philip Harkins, *Blackburn's Headhunters* (New York: W. W. Norton & Company, Inc., 1955); and John Toland, *But Not In Shame* (New York: Random House, 1961).

On the Japanese side of the picture, the testimony of General Homma and his officers at Homma's trial is perhaps most useful. Through the kindness of Mr. John H. Skeen, Jr., Homma's chief defense counsel, I have been able to supplement this with material from a collection of narrative documents written in English by Homma in 1945 for the American legal officers assigned to defend him.

A number of official Japanese reports on the Philippine campaign—some prepared during the war, some afterwards at the direction of the American Army—contain useful information. Especially interesting is a collection of personal notes written by General Homma in February and March 1942 and reflecting his thoughts and apprehensions about the fighting on Bataan. These documents, as well as other Japanese material on the Philippine campaign, are on file in the Office of Military History. A few other pertinent Japanese reports and documents, translated during the war by the Allied Translator and Interpreter Section (ATIS), General Headquarters, Southwest Pacific Area, are available in the World War II Records Division of the National Archives.

Much helpful and suggestive material on the Japanese character and military system is contained in a series of studies prepared by ATIS and organized under the general heading of "Japanese Military Psychology" (ATIS Research Report No. 76, April, 1944–October, 1945). These studies, including considerable illustrative material obtained through interrogations or the translations of captured Japanese diaries and other documents, are filed in the World War II Records Division, National Archives.

I have also drawn on such standard works as Ruth Benedict, *The Chrysanthemum and the Sword* (Boston: Houghton Mifflin Company, 1946); John F. Embree, *The Japanese Nation* (New York: Farrar & Rinehart, 1945); Hillis Lory, *Japan's Military Masters* (New York: The Viking Press, 1943); and G. B. Sansom, *Japan: A Short Cultural History* (rev. ed.; New York: Appleton-Century-Crofts, Inc., 1943). Particularly revealing of the Japanese military system in World War II and of life in the Japanese army are two novels by former soldiers: Hiroshi Noma, *Zone of Emptiness* (Cleveland and New York: The World Publishing Company, 1956), and Hanama Tasaki, *Long the Imperial Way* (Boston: Houghton Mifflin Company, 1950). Also useful on this subject were personal conversations that I held with veterans of the Japanese Army and Navy during two years I spent as an army historian in Japan.

Index

INDEX

256